LEARNING TAGALOG

Fluency Made Fast and Easy

Second Edition

Course Book 1

Frederik and Fiona De Vos

LearningTagalog.com

Copyright © 2012 Frederik and Fiona De Vos

All rights reserved.

Second Edition

ISBN 978-3-902909-03-9

Title of the First Edition (2011):
Learning Tagalog: A Complete Course with Audio, Volume 1

Complete Course Set (Course Books, Workbooks, Grammar Book, Course Audio)
ISBN 978-3-902909-07-7

Course Books
ISBN 978-3-902909-03-9 (Course Book 1)
ISBN 978-3-902909-04-6 (Course Book 2)
ISBN 978-3-902909-05-3 (Course Book 3)

Workbooks
ISBN 978-3-902909-00-8 (Workbook 1)
ISBN 978-3-902909-01-5 (Workbook 2)
ISBN 978-3-902909-02-2 (Workbook 3)

Grammar Book (Essential Tagalog Grammar, Second Edition)
ISBN 978-90-815135-4-8 (small paperback)

Course Audio
ISBN 978-3-902909-06-0 (6 Audio CDs + 1 MP3 CD)
Also available as MP3 downloads on LearningTagalog.com

Learning Tagalog (LearningTagalog.com)
team@learningtagalog.com

Cover design by John Arce.

Contents

Preface	5
Acknowledgements	7
Introduction	9
Goal of the course	11
Method	12
How to use this course	15
How to use the audio recordings	17
What you will learn	18
Lessons 1–20	21
Lesson 1 Ang bakasyon	23
Lesson 2 Ang almusal	35
Lesson 3 Kumusta?	45
Lesson 4 Sa jeep	55
Lesson 5 Ang mga alaga'	67
Lesson 6 Ang sapatos	79
Lesson 7 May sulat	89
Lesson 8 Sa fruit stand	99
Lesson 9 Ang pamilya ko	111
Lesson 10 Alas kwatro na	123
Lesson 11 Sa sala	133
Lesson 12 Ang bisita	143
Lesson 13 May tawag sa telepono	155
Lesson 14 Tanghalian sa restaurant	165
Lesson 15 Sa parlor	175
Lesson 16 Nandito na sina Tita Amy	187
Lesson 17 Sa hotel	197
Lesson 18 Ang init!	209
Lesson 19 May sakit ang asawa ko	221
Lesson 20 Sa mall	231
Quick References	241
Summary of markers and pronouns	243
Order of enclitic words	245

Preface

It began in the Philippines in 2007. Fiona and I, both freelance translators at the time, had just moved to Los Baños. Since Tagalog was now a part of my everyday life, I set out to really learn the language. I bought some books and started to learn it on my own as I had done with other languages in the past.

But this time, it was different. Tagalog was different in many ways – not difficult, just very different. In fact, Tagalog is easier than English in many respects, once you understand how it works.

As I progressed, I found that the materials I used lacked some essential information. This prompted me to develop a basic online Tagalog course that would include all the elements I often missed while learning Tagalog.

These elements are:

- dialogues for context and drills for practice
- audio recordings paired with pronunciation marks in the text
- literal and natural translations
- cultural and grammatical notes in the lessons, and a grammar reference for a complete overview
- a well-thought-out structure that introduces useful material early on while still being easy to follow

In other words, I wanted to offer a course that is "complete," in that it provides sufficient information to gain a good understanding of the language and to be able to speak it fluently.

Over the next two years, I wrote and rewrote the dialogues, based on what I heard around me. During that time, Fiona didn't get involved that much. She just answered my questions.

After several failed attempts at producing good audio recordings at home for the dialogues, we decided to use a recording studio.

For Fiona, this was a sign that the project wasn't a hobby anymore and she got fully involved.

We then practically rewrote half of the stories together in preparation for the studio recordings. In the meantime, we had moved back to Europe. After the recordings in Vienna with Fiona's brother, Ralph, we retranslated the stories and further developed the online interface.

Fiona gathered all the grammar resources she could find to write explanations for the course. This proved to be a long and painstaking process of reading, or rather dissecting, linguistics papers and *Tagalog Reference Grammar* by Schachter and Otanes, among other resources.

The fruits of this intense period were an online course and a grammar reference, which were both released in February 2010 on *LearningTagalog.com*.

Spurred on by the enthusiasm and feedback of the learners, we continued to improve the course and the grammar, and added new materials.

Now, two years later, Learning Tagalog has grown into a fully integrated suite of Tagalog learning materials: a course (online, books, ebooks), a grammar book (online, book, ebook), workbooks (books, ebooks), course audio (CDs, MP3s), free videos and free downloads.

All our Tagalog materials have been created with one goal in mind: to get you to speak Tagalog fluently in a fast, fun and easy way.

I wish you the time of your life learning and speaking Tagalog!

Frederik De Vos
July 2012

Acknowledgements

The authors would like to thank

- **Ralph de Ocampo** for the recordings
- **Alfred de Ocampo** for the first set of recordings
- **Al Rio** for the illustrations
- **Benjamin Martin** for his many suggestions regarding the online course and the print version
- **Dr. Michael E. Steele** for his many insightful questions and great suggestions regarding the course material, and for the subtitle of the second edition
- **The users of the online course** on *LearningTagalog.com* for their useful input and great feedback

Introduction

Goal of the course

The goal of this course is simple:

| To get you to speak Tagalog fluently in a fast, fun and easy way. |

The course will get you to the point where you can understand and participate in everyday Tagalog conversations.

Method

This course teaches Tagalog by example and repetition, using natural dialogues and drills taken from everyday life in the Philippines.

Natural dialogues

The advantage of using natural dialogues is that they teach you the "whole" language in its cultural context with all its nuances, emotions, typical expressions and choice of words, all of which depend on the situation. The stories are engaging and easy to relate to. As a result, you will be able to apply what you learn intuitively in your own life.

Drills

The sentence patterns in the stories are reinforced and expanded in the drills. The drills also introduce new vocabulary and related expressions.

Build-up, repetition and overlap

The lessons have been carefully designed to introduce new material little by little in order of importance. There is some degree of repetition and overlap, which allows you to recall and reinforce what you have already learned.

After having immersed yourself in the hundreds of sentences in the course, you will get a feel for how Tagalog works, and you will be able to build your own sentences intuitively.

Audio recordings

The audio recordings are an important part of the course. Together with the pronunciation marks in the text, they will help you to learn the correct pronunciation by repeating the sentences out loud.

Furthermore, the natural intonation in the recordings will help you better understand and remember the sentences.

Literal and natural translations

The meaning of each Tagalog word or group of words is presented in the literal translations, in a matching color. The literal translations are only attempts at capturing the exact meaning of the words. Sometimes, there is no corresponding word in English, and then a descriptive hint is presented between square brackets. The literal translations also help you understand the structure of the sentences. They help to bridge the gap between Tagalog and English.

The natural translations convey the same meaning as the Tagalog, in natural-sounding English, without straying too far from the original Tagalog text.

The translations in the course are not the only possible translations.

Notes and references to the grammar

The lesson notes provide concise explanations about Tagalog grammar, cultural points or the use of certain words. They are necessary to take the guesswork out of the learning process.

The notes also point to chapters in *Essential Tagalog Grammar: A Reference for Learners of Tagalog* (ETG), which provides useful tables, examples and explanations in a simple and clear format.

In references to ETG, two page numbers are provided. The first page number corresponds to the small paperback and small ebook editions, while the second corresponds to the hardcover, large paperback and large ebook editions.

Workbooks

The exercises in the workbooks are an ideal way to practice the vocabulary and sentence patterns you have learned in the lessons. They also allow you to check your progress.

An answer key is provided at the end of each workbook.

How to use this course

This course was intended to be taken in the order in which the lessons are presented.

We recommend setting aside 15 to 30 minutes per day for your Tagalog practice. At that pace, you can complete the course in about 6 months. How fast you progress depends entirely on you. Only advance as fast as you feel comfortable, and don't worry if you get set back during busier times.

The audio recordings are an important part of the course. Listen to them frequently, as they will help you memorize the material.

Doing the exercises in the workbooks will allow you to practice what you have learned. You might want to review the corresponding lesson at least a second time before doing the exercises.

The grammar reference will come in handy whenever you need an overview of a particular topic. You'll find it a useful resource, even after you have completed the course.

Advice for beginners

A lesson might provide too much information for a single day. Therefore, it may be best to split up a lesson over more than one day, as follows:

Day 1: Read the story for the first time
Day 2: Repeat the story and read the drills for the first time
Day 3: Review the whole lesson

In any case, we recommend studying a lesson for two days before moving on to the next. Alternatively, you can do two sessions on the same day if you want to advance more quickly.

Review is important. It's a good idea to review previous lessons every 5 lessons by listening to the audio and following along in the lesson overview. There will be reminders at the end of Lessons 10, 15, 20 and so on.

Give yourself some time to get used to the language. It may take a few weeks before you start getting a feel for it. Until that point, you may find it hard to build correct sentences. This is completely normal. Eventually, after repeating hundreds of sentences in this course, your mind will have built the necessary mental connections to make sense of the language and feel at home with it.

Advice for intermediate learners

Go through the first lessons as fast as you feel comfortable. Be sure not to skip anything completely because some important topics are covered early on.

As you start to encounter more new material, you may want to slow down and split a lesson over two or three days (or over two or three sessions on the same day).

Advice for advanced learners

You might want to take the whole course as a refresher, skimming the parts you find too easy. However, we recommend reading the notes as they may contain interesting pointers to grammar topics.

Listening to the audio recordings while reading along on the overview pages is a good way to reactivate your knowledge. When there is something you don't understand, you can go to that particular phrase in the lesson to find out more about it.

Reading selected chapters in ETG will surely deepen your knowledge. As an exercise after reading a chapter, you can cover the English translations of the examples and translate the Tagalog sentences or the other way around.

How to use the audio recordings

The course audio is provided as downloadable MP3 files and as a set of 6 audio CDs and 1 MP3 CD.

As the natural-speed recordings may be too fast in the beginning, a digitally slowed-down version of the recordings is included. Using the slower version might be best when you read a lesson for the first time. The natural-speed recordings could then be used for review.

The downloadable MP3 files contain one phrase each. That is, each lesson consists of about 20 MP3 files in a separate folder. This way, you can easily create a playlist for each lesson.

On the audio CDs, each track corresponds to a lesson. Track 1 corresponds to Lesson 1 and so on. There are 3 CDs containing the natural-speed recordings and 3 CDs containing the slowed-down version of the recordings. On the MP3 CD, the MP3s are provided in two formats: one lesson per MP3 and one phrase per MP3.

The most effective way to train your pronunciation and aid your memory is to repeat the sentences out loud. Also, try to mimic the intonation and emotions in the recordings. This will make you more spontaneous and will help you express what you feel in Tagalog naturally.

What you will learn

Lessons 1–20 (this book)

- pronunciation
- greetings and common expressions
- all pronouns
- to go somewhere, to be somewhere (or not)
- expressing that something exists (or not)
- to have something (or not)
- expressing how things are (or not)
- some adjective intensifiers
- expressing that something is intended for someone or something
- basic verbs, vocabulary and sentence patterns
- polite speech
- buying something
- introducing people, pets and things
- days, months, past, future, telling the time
- giving directions
- questions
- expressing likes, dislikes, wants and needs
- numbers, prices and counting
- comparing things
- expressing agreement, doubt, wonder and other emotions or nuances
- **na**, **pa**, **naman**, **pala**, **yata'** and other enclitic particles
- cultural insights through situations and dialogues
- about 30 verbs*

Lessons 21–40 (Course Book 2)

- verbs, verb affixes and their aspects
- **-um-, mag-, ma-, maka-, makapag-, -in, maki-, i-, -an, magpa-, pa-...-in, pa-...-an, ipa-, ipag-, makipag-**. Some of these verb affixes have different meanings depending on the verb.
- complex sentences with clauses

- more vocabulary and expressions
- further consolidation of material from Lessons 1–20
- cultural insights through situations and dialogues
- over 90 new verbs*

Lessons 41–60 (Course Book 3)

- more verb affixes: **ika-, mag-...-an/han, mang-** (At this point, you will know how verb affixes and aspects work, and you will be able to learn new ones easily.)
- recently completed aspect
- noun affixes
- adjective affixes
- ordinal numbers, other number expressions, dates
- sentence patterns used in written Tagalog and formal spoken Tagalog
- more vocabulary and expressions
- further consolidation of material from Lessons 1–40
- cultural insights through situations and dialogues
- over 55 new verbs*

* You will learn over 175 roots combined with various affixes. You will also learn how to use pseudo-verbs; **may, mayroon/me̱ron, mara̱mi** and **wala'** (for "to have," "there is/are/was/were (not)" etc.), and verbless "to be" sentences.

Lessons 1–20

Lesson 1
Ang bakasyon

Listen to the audio and repeat each phrase out loud a few times. In the story, Mark and Linda talk about their vacations.

A 01

Ang bakasyon

The vacation

The vacation

> The Tagalog phrase on the first line is translated literally on the second line and highlighted in a matching color. The third line gives a natural translation of the whole sentence. Literal and natural translations will help you understand how Tagalog works.

A 02

Kumusta?

How are you?

How are you?

Kumusta means *how is/are/was/were (…)*. By itself, it is used as a greeting: *How are you?*

You can simply listen to the audio for the pronunciation and read the pointers in the notes. For an overview, watch the pronunciation videos at learningtagalog.com/videos, or read the pronunciation chapter in the grammar (ETG p. 17/15).

A 03

Ma<u>bu</u>ti. Ikaw?

Good. You?

Fine. (And) you?

Ma<u>bu</u>ti means *fine, good* or *well*.

In this course, underlined syllables are stressed, that is, the vowel in the syllable is long. Optional reading: Long vowels (stress) (ETG p. 21/18).*

The /i/ in the final syllable of native Tagalog words can be pronounced as /e/ when followed by a pause, like in **ma<u>bu</u>ti**.

* The page number depends on the edition. See p. 13.

A 04

Ma**bu**ti **rin**.

Good *too.*

I'm fine too.

Rin (or **din**) means *too, also* or *either*. **Rin** is commonly used after words ending in a vowel. **Din** is commonly used after words ending in a consonant. However, this rule is not strict.

A 05

Kumusta **ang** bakasyon **mo**?

How was *the* *vacation* *your?*

How was your vacation?

This is a very typical sentence pattern in Tagalog. You'll soon get used to it.

A 06

Masaya. **Pumunta** ako **sa** Ba**na**ue.

Fun. *Went* *I* *to* *Banaue.*

It was fun. I went to Banaue.

Masaya – *happy, fun*. **Sa** can mean *to, on, at, into, onto, through* etc.

A 07

Wow! Maganda ba ang Rice Terraces?

Wow! Beautiful [question] the Rice Terraces?

Wow! Are the Rice Terraces beautiful?

Ba turns a statement into a question. It often follows the first word of the sentence.

A 08

Oo, ang ganda talaga!

Yes, very beautiful really!

Yes, very beautiful!

Ganda – *beauty*.

Ang can be added to a quality (e.g. **ganda**) to mean *how (…)* or *very (…)*. **Ang ganda!** – *How pretty!* This **ang** is different from the **ang** in the previous sentence, which means *the*.

A 09

Ikaw, kumusta ang bakasyon mo?

You, how was the vacation your?

(And) you, how was your vacation?

26 Learning Tagalog: Fluency Made Fast and Easy

A 10

Masaya rin.
Pumunta ako sa London, sa New York at sa Sydney.

Fun too.
Went I to London, to New York and to Sydney.

It was fun too. I went to London, New York and Sydney.

Masaya – *happy* or *fun (adjective).*

Saya – *happiness* or *fun (noun).*

In **masaya**, **saya** is the root, which carries the core meaning of the word. **Ma-** is an affix, which means *having (a certain quality)* or *having a lot of (something).*

Optional reading: Roots and affixes (ETG p. 29/25).

A 11

Talaga?

Really?

Really?

A 12

Joke lang. Nasa bahay lang ako.

Joke only. Was at home only I.

Just kidding. I just stayed home.

Nasa is used to indicate where someone or something is. It is equivalent to *is/are/was/were in/on/at* etc. **Nasa Cebu** – *is in Cebu;* **nasa mesa** / **nasa lamesa** – *is on (the) table.*

Drills

B 01

Pumunta ako sa Maynila'.

Went I to Manila.

I went to Manila.

> Notice the /'/ at the end of **Maynila'**. In this course, the symbol /'/ is used to indicate either (1) a glottal stop, when it is followed by a pause; or (2) a long vowel, when immediately followed by another word.
>
> An example of a glottal stop in English is the sound represented by the hyphen in *uh-oh*!
>
> Optional reading: Final glottal stops (ETG p. 22/20).

B 02

Masaya ba ang bakasyon mo?

Happy [question] the vacation your?

Did you have fun on your vacation? (Was your vacation fun?)

B 03

Oo, ang saya talaga!

Yes, very happy really!

Yes, I had a great time! (It was really fun!)

B 04

Kumusta ang pamilya mo?

How is the family your?

How is your family?

B 05

Mabuti.

Good.

Fine.

The root of **mabuti** is **buti** (*goodness*).

B 06

Salamat.

Thank you.

Thank you.

B 07

Thank you.

Thank you.

Thank you.

B 08

Pa<u>sen</u>sya na.

Patience now.

Sorry.

B 09

Sorry.

Sorry.

Sorry.

B 10

Ingat.

Take care.

Take care.

The lesson overview on the next page allows you to review the whole lesson one more time. Listen to the recordings and try to understand everything.

You might want to do the same lesson for two days before moving on to the next lesson.

The key to success in learning Tagalog is daily practice. By setting aside 15 to 30 minutes a day, you will be amazed at the progress you are making.

Ang bakasyon

Kumusta?
Ma<u>bu</u>ti. Ikaw?
Ma<u>bu</u>ti rin.
Kumusta ang bakasyon mo?
Masaya. Pumunta ako sa Ba<u>na</u>ue.
Wow! Maganda ba ang Rice Terraces?
<u>O</u>o, ang ganda talaga!
Ikaw, kumusta ang bakasyon mo?
Masaya rin. Pumunta ako sa London, sa New York at sa Sydney.
Talaga?
Joke lang. <u>Na</u>sa <u>ba</u>hay lang ako.

Drills

Pumunta ako sa May<u>ni</u>la'.
Masaya ba ang bakasyon mo?
<u>O</u>o, ang saya talaga!
Kumusta ang pa<u>mi</u>lya mo?
Ma<u>bu</u>ti.
Sa<u>la</u>mat.
Thank you.
Pa<u>sen</u>sya na.
Sorry.
<u>I</u>ngat.

Lesson 2
Ang almusal

Breakfast is served. Don't worry if you forget words at first. You will come across them again.

A 01

Ang almusal

The breakfast

The breakfast

> If you prefer to split up a lesson over two days, you can print out the Course Progress Sheet to record your progress. You can download it at learningtagalog.com/downloads.html.

A 02

Maraming pagkain sa lamesa.

There is a lot of-[linker] food on table.

There's a lot of food on the table.

Marami can mean *there is/are/was/were a lot of (…)*.

The ending **-ng** is used to link **marami** and **pagkain** *(food)*.

Optional reading: **Na/-ng** (ETG p. 34/29).

A 03

May kanin at ulam.

There is cooked rice and dish that goes with rice.

There's rice and a dish that goes with it.

In this sentence, **may** means *there is/are/was/were (a/some) (…)*.

Ulam is what is eaten with rice, such as fish.

A 04

May gulay at prutas.

There are vegetable and fruit.

There are vegetables and fruits.

> Fruits and vegetables are uncountable in Tagalog, just like meat or sugar in English.

A 05

May isda', itlog at karne.

There are fish, egg and meat.

There are fish, eggs and meat.

A 06

May tubig, pero walang juice.

There is water, but there is no-[linker] juice.

There's water, but there's no juice.

> **Walang juice** means *there's no juice*. **Wala'** is linked to **juice** with the linker **-ng**.

A 07

Ma͟alat ang isda'.

Salty the fish.

The fish is salty.

This sentence illustrates the basic sentence pattern of Tagalog: [News][Point of Departure]. The Point of Departure (POD) is the starting point of the sentence. It is the object, person, idea etc. that the speaker thinks about before he or she begins the sentence, and that he or she assumes the listener knows. The News is the relatively new information that is given about the POD.

Recommended reading: The POD and the News (ETG p. 35/31).

A 08

Mapait ang gamot.

Bitter the medicine.

The medicine is bitter.

Ang gamot is the POD in this sentence.

A 09

Matamis ang mangga, pero maasim ang pinya.

Sweet the mango, but sour the pineapple.

The mango is sweet, but the pineapple is sour.

> In this sentence, both **ang mangga** and **ang pinya** are PODs.

A 10

Malamig ang tubig, pero mainit ang kape.

Cold the water, but hot the coffee.

The water is cold, but the coffee is hot.

A 11

Masarap ang almusal.

Tasty the breakfast.

The breakfast is tasty.

> **Ang**, which is often translated as *the*, is a marker. Markers are short words that indicate the role of a word in a sentence.
>
> Recommended reading: Ang markers (ETG p. 43/37) and Uses of Ang markers (ETG p. 45/39).

Drills

B 01

Maraming prutas sa lamesa.

There is a lot of-[linker] fruit on table.

There's a lot of fruit on the table.

B 02

Walang gulay sa lamesa.

There are no-[linker] vegetable on table.

There are no vegetables on the table.

B 03

Maalat ang itlog.

Salty the egg.

The egg is salty.

B 04

Matamis ito.

Sweet this.

This is sweet.

> **Ito** – *this (near me)*. In this sentence, **ito** is the POD.

B 05

Mapait iyan.

Bitter that (near you).

That is bitter.

> **Iyan** – *that (near you)*.

B 06

Maasim iyon.

Sour that (over there).

That is sour.

> **Iyon** – *that (over there, far from you and me)*.

B 07

isdang ma̱alat

fish-[linker] salty

fish that is salty

B 08

pagka̱ing masarap

food-[linker] tasty

food that tastes good

B 09

gamot na mapait

medicine [linker] bitter

medicine that is bitter

> **Na** is used as a linker instead of **-ng**, because **gamot** ends in a consonant other than /**n**/. **-ng** is used when the first word ends in a vowel or /**n**/.

B 10

maalat na isda'

salty [linker] fish

salty fish

B 11

masarap na pagkain

tasty [linker] food

tasty food

B 12

mapait na gamot

bitter [linker] medicine

bitter medicine

> In this lesson, the focus was on the basic sentence structure. It's quite normal to feel confused at first. Tagalog is probably very different from the language(s) you speak. Take your time and review the phrases until they sound familiar. In a few lessons, you will start to get a feel for how Tagalog works.

Ang almusal

Maraming pagkain sa lamesa.
May kanin at ulam.
May gulay at prutas.
May isda', itlog at karne.
May tubig, pero walang juice.
Maalat ang isda'.
Mapait ang gamot.
Matamis ang mangga, pero maasim ang pinya.
Malamig ang tubig, pero mainit ang kape.
Masarap ang almusal.

Drills

Maraming prutas sa lamesa.
Walang gulay sa lamesa.
Maalat ang itlog.
Matamis ito.
Mapait iyan.
Maasim iyon.
isdang maalat
pagkaing masarap
gamot na mapait
maalat na isda'
masarap na pagkain
mapait na gamot

Lesson 3
Kumusta?

Two students meet on the street after class.

A 01

Kumusta?

How are you?

How are you?

A 02

Hello!

Hello!

Hello!

A 03

Hello, kumusta?

Hello, how are you?

Hello, how are you?

A 04

Ma<u>bu</u>ti. Ikaw?

Good. You?

Fine. (And) you?

A 05

Ma<u>bu</u>ti rin.

Good too.

I'm fine too.

A 06

Saan ka pupunta?

Where you will go?

Where are you going?

Ikaw and ka both mean *you*. Ikaw is generally used in the News of a sentence, while ka is used in the POD. Don't worry, you'll soon pick up the patterns!

A 07

Sa klase ko. Ikaw, may klase ka ba ngayon?

To class my. You, have class you [question] now?

To my class. How about you? Do you have a class now?

In this sentence, **may** means *has/have/had (a/some) (...)*. **May klase ka.** – *You have a class.* **Ka** is the POD.

Notice the pronunciation of **may** here. It sounds like *"mey."* The sound /ay/ can be pronounced as *"ay," "ey"* or *"e."*

Optional reading: Replaceable sounds (ETG p. 25/22).

A 08

**Wala' na. Tapos na.
Bukas ang sunod na klase ko.**

Have none now. Done now.
Tomorrow the next [linker] class my.

Not anymore. I'm done. My next class is tomorrow.

Note the pronunciation of **Wala' na**. Since **wala'** is immediately followed by another word **(na)**, the final vowel is long and there is no glottal stop.

In this sentence, **wala'** means *has/have/had no (…)* or *has/have/had none*.

Recommended reading: **May, mayroon/meron, marami, wala'**: Overview (ETG p. 379/341).

A 09

O sige. Magkita' na lang tayo bukas.

OK. Meet just we (incl. you) tomorrow.

OK. Let's just see each other tomorrow.

Magkita' is a verb in the basic form (the form one would find in a dictionary, usually under the verb root).

Basic form + **tayo**. – *Let's (…)*. **Magkita' tayo** – *Let's meet*.

Tayo – *we (including you)*. **Kami** – *we (excluding you)*.

A 10

Sige, ingat.

OK, take care.

All right, take care.

A 11

Ingat din.

Take care too.

You too (take care).

Drills

B 01

May trab<u>a</u>ho ka ba ngayon?

Have work you [question] today?

Do you have work today?

B 02

M<u>e</u>ron. May trab<u>a</u>ho ako <u>a</u>raw-<u>a</u>raw.

Have some. Have work I every day.

Yes. I have work every day.

Yes/no questions starting with **may**, **m<u>e</u>ron** or **wala'** are generally answered with **m<u>e</u>ron** (for *yes*) or **wala'** (for *no*).

Optional reading: Stand-alone **m<u>e</u>ron/mar<u>a</u>mi/wala'** (ETG p. 381/343).

B 03

Ako rin.

I too.

Me too.

B 04

May meeting ka ba ka<u>ni</u>na?

Had meeting you [question] earlier today?

Did you have a meeting earlier today?

B 05

M<u>e</u>ron.

Had one.

Yes (I did).

B 06

May meeting ka ba <u>ma</u>maya'?

Have meeting you [question] later today?

Do you have a meeting later today?

B 07

M<u>e</u>ron din.

Have one too.

Yes, I do, as well.

B 08

May p̲asok ka ba kah̲apon?

Had work/school you [question] yesterday?

Did you have work/school yesterday?

B 09

Wala'.

Had none.

No.

B 10

May p̲asok ka ba b̲ukas?

Have work/school you [question] tomorrow?

Do you have work/school tomorrow?

B 11

Wala' rin.

Have none either.

No, I don't either.

Kumusta?

Hello!
Hello, kumusta?
Ma<u>bu</u>ti. Ikaw?
Ma<u>bu</u>ti rin.
Saan ka <u>pu</u>punta?
Sa <u>kla</u>se ko. Ikaw, may <u>kla</u>se ka ba ngayon?
Wala' na. Tapos na. <u>Bu</u>kas ang sunod na <u>kla</u>se ko.
O sige. Mag<u>ki</u>ta' na lang <u>ta</u>yo <u>bu</u>kas.
Sige, <u>i</u>ngat.
<u>I</u>ngat din.

Drills

May tra<u>ba</u>ho ka ba ngayon?
<u>Me</u>ron. May tra<u>ba</u>ho ako <u>a</u>raw-<u>a</u>raw.
Ako rin.
May meeting ka ba ka<u>ni</u>na?
<u>Me</u>ron.
May meeting ka ba <u>ma</u>maya'?
<u>Me</u>ron din.
May <u>pa</u>sok ka ba ka<u>ha</u>pon?
Wala'.
May <u>pa</u>sok ka ba <u>bu</u>kas?
Wala' rin.

Lesson 4
Sa jeep

A woman goes to the market by jeepney. She's new in town and asks the driver for directions.

A 01

Sa jeep

On jeepney

On the jeepney

A 02

Bayad.

Payment.

Here's my fare.

Bayad is often said when handing one's fare on a jeepney.

A 03

Ilan?

How many?

(For) how many (people)?

A 04

Isa lang.

One only.

Just one.

A 05

Saan kayo bababa'?

Where you (polite) will go down?

Where will you get off?

Sometimes, the driver needs to know where the passenger will get off to determine the fare.

Kayo, *you (plural)*, is used instead of **ikaw/ka**, *you (singular)*, to address older people, superiors, adult strangers and adult customers.

A 06

Sa bayan.

In town.

In town.

Bayan – *town, town center.*

A 07

Eto ang sukli'.

Here is the change.

Here's the change.

Sukli' means *change (money)*.

Eto (or **eto**) means *here is/are* (when introducing or pointing to someone or something).

Optional reading: **Eto, ayan, ayun** (ETG p. 293/263).

A 08

Salamat. […]

Thanks. […]

Thanks. […]

A 09

Malayo' pa ba ang palengke?

Far still [question] the market?

Is the market still far?

Here, **pa** means *still*.

A 10

Hindi', mal_a_pit na.

No, near now.

No, we're almost there.

A 11

Malaki ba ang pal_e_ngke r_i_to?

Big [question] the market here?

Is the market here big?

R_i_to or **d_i_to** means *here*.

A 12

_O_o. [...]

Yes. [...]

Yes. [...]

A 13

Nandito na ang palengke.

Is here now the market.

We're at the market now. (The market is here now.)

Nandito means *is/are/was/were here*.

A 14

Sige, salamat.

OK, thanks.

OK, thanks.

Drills

B 01

Malapit na ang palengke.

Near now the market.

We're near the market now. (The market is near now.)

B 02

Malayo' pa ang bayan.

Far still the town.

The town is still far.

B 03

Mahal ang gulay sa supermarket.

Expensive the vegetable at supermarket.

The vegetables at the supermarket are expensive.

> **Mahal** is the root itself. It does not have a **ma-** affix like many other adjectives.

B 04

Mura ang gulay sa palengke.

Cheap the vegetable at market.

The vegetables at the market are cheap.

B 05

Maraming gulay dito.

There are a lot of-[linker] vegetable here.

There are a lot of vegetables here.

B 06

Walang prutas diyan.

There is no-[linker] fruit there (near you).

There's no fruit there (near you).

> **Diyan** or **riyan** means *there (near you)*.

B 07

Wala' ring prutas doon.

There is no either-[linker] fruit over there.

There's no fruit over there either.

Doon or **roon** means *over there (far from you and me).*

The linker **-ng** in **walang prutas** is moved after **rin** in this sentence: **Wala' ring prutas.** The reason is that **din/rin** is an enclitic word. Enclitic words are words that generally follow either the first word of the sentence or another enclitic word. When enclitic words come between linked words, **na/-ng** is moved to the last enclitic word.

B 08

Bayad.

Payment.

Here's my fare.

B 09

Para.

Stop.

Please stop. (I want to get off.)

On a jeepney, you say **para** to let the driver know you want to get off.

B 10

isa, dalawa, tatlo, apat, lima

one, two, three, four, five

one, two, three, four, five

B 11

anim, pito, walo, siyam, sampu'

six, seven, eight, nine, ten

six, seven, eight, nine, ten

Sa jeep

B̲ayad.
Ilan?
Isa lang.
Saan kayo b̲ababa'?
Sa b̲ayan.
E̲to ang sukli'.
Sal̲amat. [...]
Mal̲ayo' pa ba ang pal̲engke?
Hindi', mal̲apit na.
Malaki ba ang pal̲engke r̲ito?
O̲o. [...]
Nand̲ito na ang pal̲engke.
Sige, sal̲amat.

Drills

Mal̲apit na ang pal̲engke.
Mal̲ayo' pa ang b̲ayan.
Mahal ang g̲ulay sa supermarket.
M̲ura ang g̲ulay sa pal̲engke.
Mar̲aming g̲ulay d̲ito.
Walang pr̲utas diyan.
Wala' ring pr̲utas doon.
B̲ayad.
P̲ara.
isa, dalawa, tatlo, a̲pat, lima
a̲nim, pito, walo, siyam, sampu'

Lesson 5
Ang mga al<u>a</u>ga'

Cindy introduces her dogs, Tabby and Tingting, to her new neighbor.

A 01

Ang mga al<u>a</u>ga'

The [plural] pet

The pets

Noun plurals are formed by placing **mga** before the noun.

A 02

Ito si Tabby, ang aso ko.

This [Ang marker] Tabby, the dog my.

This is my dog Tabby.

Ito, si Tabby and **ang aso** are all examples of Ang phrases. They can assume the same roles in a sentence. Ang phrases can either be Ang pronouns or phrases introduced by an Ang marker. The POD is always expressed as an Ang phrase.

Take a moment to look at the Summary of markers and pronouns in the Quick References on p. 243 (or ETG p. 68/59). All these markers and pronouns will be covered in the next lessons.

A 03

A, hello Tabby! Bakit Tabby ang pangalan niya?

Ah, hello Tabby! Why Tabby the name his/her?

Ah, hello Tabby! Why is he called Tabby? (Why is his name Tabby?)

A 04

Kasi ang taba' niya e.

Because *very fat* *of him/her* *you see.*

Because he's so fat.

When **ang** is used as an intensifier (**ang** + root, as in: **ang taba'** – *how fat, very fat*), the person or thing described is expressed as a Ng phrase (**niya** in this case).

As we will see later, there are other intensifiers that follow the same pattern.

A 05

Oo nga' ano. Mataba' nga' siya.

Yes, *indeed* *isn't it.* *Fat* *indeed* *he/she.*

Yes, now that you said it. He's fat indeed.

Oo nga' ano. – *Yes, now that you said it.* It's an expression (translated loosely to capture the same meaning).

Mataba' siya – *he/she's fat.* **Ang taba' niya** – *he/she's very fat* (see the previous phrase). **Siya** is an Ang pronoun and **niya** is the corresponding Ng pronoun. You can check the Summary of markers and pronouns again on p. 243 (or ETG p. 68/59).

A 06

Ang bait niya di ba?

Very nice of him/her right?

He's very nice, isn't he?

Di ba – *isn't it/he/she, aren't they etc.*

Mabait siya – *he/she's nice.* **Ang bait niya** – *he/she's very nice.*

A 07

Oo. Ilang taon na siya?

Yes. How many-[linker] year now he/she?

Yes. How old is he? (How many years is he?)

Ilang taon na – *how old.*

A 08

Tatlong taon na yata'. […]

Three-[linker] year now maybe. […]

Three years, I think. […]

Yata' is used to express uncertainty, so it can mean *I think, I guess, maybe, if I remember correctly* etc.

A 09

At ito naman si Tingting, ang kapatid ni Tabby.

And this [contrast] [Ang marker] Tingting, the sibling of Tabby.

And this is Tingting, Tabby's sister (sibling).

> **Naman** can be used to show contrast with what has been previously introduced.

A 10

Ang payat ni Tingting!

How thin of Tingting!

Tingting is so thin!

> **Payat si Tingting** – *Tingting is thin.* **Payat** is an adjective without an affix. **Ang payat ni Tingting** – *Tingting is very/so thin.*

A 11

Parang tingting di ba?

Like midrib (leaf vein) right?

As thin as a twig, isn't she?

A **tingting** is the midrib (central vein) of a palm leaf. It is often bundled together and used as a broom in the Philippines. **Tingting** can also be used to describe skinny people.

Drills

B 01

Mataba' si Tabby.

Fat [Ang marker] Tabby.

Tabby is fat.

B 02

Ang taba' ni Tabby!

How fat of Tabby!

Tabby is so fat!

B 03

Mabait si Tingting.

Nice [Ang marker] Tingting.

Tingting is nice.

B 04

Ang bait ni Tingting.

How nice of Tingting.

Tingting is so nice.

B 05

Ang bait-bait ni Tingting.

How very nice of Tingting.

Tingting is sooo nice.

> Repeating **bait** a second time intensifies its meaning even more.

B 06

Payat siya.

Thin he/she.

He/she is thin.

B 07

Ang payat niya.

How thin of him/her.

He/she is so thin.

B 08

Makulit ang aso niya.

Importunate the dog his/her.

His/her dog is irritating.

B 09

Ang kulit ng aso niya.

How importunate of dog his/her.

His/her dog is so irritating.

B 10

Maganda ito.

Beautiful this.

This is pretty.

B 11

Ang ganda nito.

How beautiful of this.

This is so pretty.

B 12

Masakit iyan.

Painful *that (near you).*

That hurts. (That's painful.)

B 13

Ang sakit niyan.

How painful *of that (near you).*

That really hurts. (That's so painful.)

B 14

Pangit iyon.

Ugly *that (over there).*

That's ugly.

B 15

Ang pangit niyon.

How ugly *of that (over there).*

That's so ugly.

Ang mga al__a__ga'

Ito si Tabby, ang __a__so ko.
A, hello Tabby! __B__akit Tabby ang pa__ng__alan niya?
Kasi ang taba' niya e.
__O__o nga' ano. Mataba' nga' siya.
Ang bait niya di ba?
__O__o. Ilang taon na siya?
Tatlong taon na __y__ata'. […]
At ito naman si Tingting, ang kapatid ni Tabby.
Ang payat ni Tingting!
__P__arang tingting di ba?

Drills

Mataba' si Tabby.
Ang taba' ni Tabby!
Mabait si Tingting.
Ang bait ni Tingting.
Ang bait-bait ni Tingting.
Payat siya.
Ang payat niya.
Makulit ang __a__so niya.
Ang kulit ng __a__so niya.
Maganda ito.
Ang ganda nito.
Masakit iyan.
Ang sakit niyan.
__P__angit iyon.
Ang __p__angit niyon.

Lesson 6
Ang sapatos

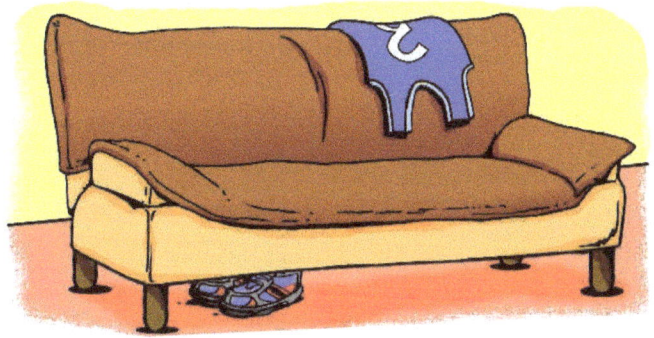

Julius is looking for his shoes. He asks his sister Mia where they are.

A 01

Ang sapatos

The shoes

The shoes

Sapatos means *shoe* or *shoes*.

A 02

Nasaan ang sapatos ko?

Where are the shoes my?

Where are my shoes?

Nasaan (...)? – *Where is/are/was/were (...)?*

Nasaan is used to ask where someone or something is. **Saan** is used to ask where something happens.

A 03

Ewan ko. Bakit? Lalabas ka ba?

Not known by me. Why? Will go out you [question]?

I don't know. Why? Are you going out?

Here, **ko** means *by me*, instead of *my*.

A 04

Oo, may basketball ako. Late na nga' ako e.

Yes, have basketball I. Late already in fact I you see.

Yes, I have basketball. And actually, I'm already late.

Na, **nga'** and **ako** are enclitic words.

A 05

Kumain ka na?

Ate you already?

Have you eaten?

Verbs will be covered in detail after Lesson 20.

A 06

Oo, tapos na.

Yes, done now.

Yes, I'm done.

Lesson 6   81

A 07

Siguro nasa sala ang sapatos mo.

Maybe are in living room the shoes your.

Maybe your shoes are in the living room.

Nasa indicates where someone or something is.

A 08

Ay, tama' ka. Alam ko na. Nasa ilalim ng sofa.

Oh, right you. Known by me now. Are in place beneath of sofa.

Oh, you're right. I know now. They're under the sofa.

Ng is a Ng marker.

A 09

Ikaw talaga...

You really...

You're really so...

Ikaw talaga – *You're really so...* or *This is so typical of you.*

A 10

Aalis na ako.

Will leave now I.

I'm off. (I'll leave now.)

A 11

Sige.

OK.

OK.

Drills

B 01

Nasaan ang payong mo?

Where is the umbrella your?

Where's your umbrella?

> **Mo** is a Ng pronoun. Ng pronouns generally have the same roles in a sentence as phrases introduced by a Ng marker.

B 02

Nasa taas.

Is in place above.

Upstairs.

> **Nasa** taas or **nasa** itaas means *upstairs, higher up* or *at the top*.

B 03

Nasa baba'.

Is in place below.

Downstairs.

Nasa baba' or **nasa ibaba'** means *downstairs, lower down* or *at the bottom.*

B 04

Nandito sa likod ng pinto'.

Is here at back of door.

It's here, behind the door.

B 05

Nandiyan sa tabi ng silya.

Is there (near you) on side of chair.

It's there, next to the chair.

Nandiyan means *is/are/was/were there (near you).*

B 06

Nandoon sa lamesa.

Is over there on table.

It's over there, on the table.

Nandoon means *is/are/was/were over there (far from you and me)*.

Optional reading: **Nandito, nandiyan, nandoon** (ETG p. 291/261).

B 07

Nasa labas yata'.

Is in outside maybe.

It's outside, I think.

B 08

Nasa loob ng kotse.

Is in inside of car.

It's in the car.

Ang sapatos

Nasaan ang sapatos ko?
Ewan ko. Bakit? Lalabas ka ba?
Oo, may basketball ako. Late na nga' ako e.
Kumain ka na?
Oo, tapos na.
Siguro nasa sala ang sapatos mo.
Ay, tama' ka. Alam ko na. Nasa ilalim ng sofa.
Ikaw talaga…
Aalis na ako.
Sige.

Drills

Nasaan ang payong mo?
Nasa taas.
Nasa baba'.
Nandito sa likod ng pinto'.
Nandiyan sa tabi ng silya.
Nandoon sa lamesa.
Nasa labas yata'.
Nasa loob ng kotse.

Lesson 7
May <u>sulat</u>

The postman brings a letter for Mr. Cruz but only his daughter is home.

A 01

May sulat

There is letter

There's a letter

A 02

Tao po'!

Person [polite]!

Anyone home?

The expression **Tao po'** is used to announce one's presence at the door or gate of a house, in the absence of a doorbell.

Po' (or **ho'**) is used for talking politely to older people, superiors, adult strangers and adult customers. It is sometimes translated as *sir* or *ma'am*.

A 03

Ano po' iyon?

What [polite] it?

Yes? (What is it?) (polite)

Iyon can also be understood as *it*.

A 04

May sulat para sa tatay mo.

There is letter for dad your.

There's a letter for your dad.

A 05

Umalis po' siya e.

Left [polite] he/she I'm afraid.

I'm afraid he's out. (I'm afraid he left.) (polite)

Po' is an enclitic word. Enclitic words are words that generally follow either the first word of the sentence or another enclitic word. The order in which enclitic words follow one another is given on p. 245.

Recommended reading: Enclitic words: Overview (ETG p. 339/305).

A 06

Nandito ba ang nanay mo?

Is here [question] the mom your?

Is your mom here (home)?

A 07

Wala' rin po' siya.

Is not here *either* *[polite]* *he/she.*

She's not here either. (polite)

Wala' can also mean *is/are/was/were not here/there*. With this meaning, **wala'** doesn't take a linker.

Rin, **po'** and **siya** are enclitic words.

A 08

**Ganoon ba? Di' bale.
Eto ang sulat para sa tatay mo.**

Like that (over there) *[question]*? *Never mind.*
Here is *the* *letter* *for* *dad* *your.*

Is that so? Never mind then. Here's the letter for your dad.

Eto is used when introducing something, handing something to someone or pointing to something (near the speaker). **Nandito**, on the other hand, is used more generally to indicate where something is.

A 09

Sige po'. Salamat po'.

OK [polite]. Thank you [polite].

OK. Thank you. (polite)

Drills

B 01

Nan<u>di</u>to ang <u>su</u>lat.

Is here the letter.

The letter is here.

B 02

Nan<u>di</u>to po' ang <u>su</u>lat.

Is here [polite] the letter.

The letter is here. (polite)

B 03

Nandiyan na si <u>Ta</u>tay.

Is there (near you) now [Ang marker] Dad.

Dad is there now. (Dad has arrived.)

Here, **Tatay** is a nickname *("Dad")* and therefore, takes **si** as a marker, not **ang**.

B 04

Nandoon ang susi'.

Is over there the key.

The key is over there.

B 05

Wala' sila sa bahay.

Are not they at home.

They aren't home.

Wala' sa is the opposite of **nasa**. **Sila** is enclitic.

Optional reading: **Wala' sa, wala' rito** (ETG p. 294/264).

B 06

Wala' po' sila sa bahay.

Are not [polite] they at home.

They aren't home. (polite)

B 07

Walang tao sa bahay.

There is no-[linker] person at home.

There's no one home.

B 08

Wala' pong tao sa bahay.

There is no [polite]-[linker] person at home.

There's no one home. (polite)

Walang tao becomes **wala' pong tao** in polite speech. **Na/-ng** is inserted after **po'**.

Optional reading: Enclitic words and **na/-ng** (ETG p. 340/306).

B 09

Wala' siya sa bahay. Nasa ospital siya.

Is not he/she at home. Is in hospital he/she.

He/she's not home. He/she's in the hospital.

B 10

Ano ang sakit niya?

What the illness his/her?

What (illness) does he/she have? (What is his/her illness?)

B 11

Wala'. Nurse siya.

Has none. Nurse he/she.

Nothing. He/she's a nurse.

B 12

Ano ang pangalan niya?

What the name his/her?

What's his/her name?

B 13

Hindi' ko alam.

Not by me known.

I don't know.

Hindi' alam – *not known.* **Ko** is enclitic.

May sulat

Tao po'!
Ano po' iyon?
May sulat para sa tatay mo.
Umalis po' siya e.
Nandito ba ang nanay mo?
Wala' rin po' siya.
Ganoon ba? Di' bale. Eto ang sulat para sa tatay mo.
Sige po'. Salamat po'.

Drills

Nandito ang sulat.
Nandito po' ang sulat.
Nandiyan na si Tatay.
Nandoon ang susi'.
Wala' sila sa bahay.
Wala' po' sila sa bahay.
Walang tao sa bahay.
Wala' pong tao sa bahay.
Wala' siya sa bahay. Nasa ospital siya.
Ano ang sakit niya?
Wala'. Nurse siya.
Ano ang pangalan niya?
Hindi' ko alam.

Lesson 8
Sa fruit stand

Mr. Lopez buys fruits from a girl at a fruit stand.

A 01

Sa fruit stand

At fruit stand

At the fruit stand

A 02

Meron ba kayong pakwan?

Have [question] you (plural)-[linker] watermelon?

Do you have watermelons?

Merong pakwan. – *There are watermelons.* **Meron ba kayong pakwan?** – *Do you have watermelons?* **Na/-ng** is inserted after **ba** and **kayo**, which are both enclitic.

To refresh your memory: **May, mayroon/meron, marami, wala'**: Overview (ETG p. 379/341).

A 03

**Wala' po'.
Pero meron kaming chico at langka'.**

*Have none [polite].
But have we (excl. you)-[linker] chico and jackfruit.*

No, sir. But we do have chico and jackfruit.

Kami – *we (excluding you).*

A 04

Magkano ang langka'?

How much the jackfruit?

How much are the jackfruits?

Magkano means *how much* and is used only for prices.

A 05

Two hundred fifty ang malaki, dalawang daan ang maliit.

Two hundred fifty the big, two-[linker] hundred the small.

The big ones are two hundred fifty, the small ones are two hundred.

Malaki – *big*. **Ang malaki** – *the big one*, or in the case of fruits, *the big ones*.

Optional reading: Verbs, adjectives etc. used as nouns (ETG p. 101/87).

A 06

Walang tawad?

There is no-[linker] discount?

Is the price negotiable? (Is there no discount?)

Walang tawad? is often used when haggling.

A 07

One hundred ninety na lang po' para sa maliit.

One hundred ninety instead [polite] for small.

Just one hundred ninety then for the small ones. (polite)

Na lang can be used to present an alternative to what has been said or planned before, or to what is expected.

Na, **lang** and **po'** are enclitic.

A 08

**Sige, pabili ng isa.
May mangga ba kayo?**

*OK, could you let me buy [Ng marker] one.
Have mango [question] you (plural)?*

OK, I'll get (buy) one. Do you have mangoes?

Pa- words indicating a request (such as **pabili**) may be followed by a Ng marker or a Ng pronoun (and not by an Ang marker or pronoun).

Meron bang mangga? But: **May mangga ba? May** cannot be immediately followed by an enclitic word such as **ba**.

A 09

O̱po'. Ilan po'?

Yes (polite). How many [polite]?

Yes. How many (would you like)? (polite)

O̱po' (or o̱ho') is the polite way of saying *yes*.

A 10

Tatlong pira̱so lang.

Three-[linker] piece only.

Just three (pieces).

A 11

Forty-five pe̱sos po'.

Forty-five pesos [polite].

That will be forty-five pesos, sir.

A 12

Magkano lahat?

How much all?

How much is it in total?

Lahat can mean *all, everything* or *everyone.*

A 13

Two hundred thirty-five po'.

Two hundred thirty-five [polite].

Two hundred thirty-five pesos, sir.

A 14

Salamat.

Thanks.

Thanks.

Drills

B 01

M̲eron silang langka'.

Have they-[linker] jackfruit.

They have jackfruits.

B 02

Wala' po' kaming pakwan.

Have no [polite] we (excl. you)-[linker] watermelon.

We don't have watermelons. (polite)

B 03

Pabili nga' po' ng mangga.

Could you let me buy please [polite] [Ng marker] mango.

I'd like to buy some mangoes, please. (polite)

> **Nga'** can be used to make a command or request more polite and friendly.

B 04

Hindi' maganda ang saging na ito.

Not pretty the banana [linker] this.

This banana doesn't look good.

Ito – *this.*

Ang saging na ito – *this banana.* **Na/-ng** is used to link **ito/iyan/iyon** with the thing it specifies.

Optional reading: This dog, that dog etc. (ETG p. 56/48).

B 05

Pangit ang pakwang ito.

Ugly the watermelon-[linker] this.

This watermelon doesn't look good.

B 06

Magkano ang pinyang iyan?

How much the pineapple-[linker] that (near you)?

How much is that pineapple?

Iyan – that (near you).

Ang pinyang iyan – that pineapple (near you).

B 07

Isang daan lang po'.

One-[linker] hundred only [polite].

Only one hundred pesos, sir.

B 08

Magkano ang isang kilong saging?

How much the one-[linker] kilo-[linker] banana?

How much is a kilo of bananas?

B 09

Sixty-five po'.

Sixty-five [polite].

Sixty-five pesos, sir.

B 10

**Wala' akong barya.
Buong limang daan lang ang pera ko.**

*Have no I-[linker] loose change.
Whole-[linker] five-[linker] hundred only the money my.*

I don't have loose change. I only have a five hundred bill. (My money is a whole five hundred only.)

Barya – *loose change* or *coins and small notes.*

Buo – *whole.*

B 11

Di' bale, may panukli' po' ako.

Never mind, have change [polite] I.

Don't worry, I have change, sir.

May cannot be followed by enclitic words, such as **po'** and **ako**.

B 12

isang daan, isang libo, isang milyon

one-[linker] hundred, one-[linker] thousand, one-[linker] million

one hundred, one thousand, one million

Sa fruit stand

M̲eron ba kayong pakwan?
Wala' po'. P̲ero m̲eron kaming ch̲ico at langka'.
Magk̲ano ang langka'?
Two hundred fifty ang malaki, dalawang daan ang maliit.
Walang t̲awad?
One hundred ninety na lang po' p̲ara sa maliit.
Sige, pabili ng isa. May mangga ba kayo?
O̲po'. Ilan po'?
Tatlong pir̲aso lang.
Forty-five p̲esos po'.
Magk̲ano lahat?
Two hundred thirty-five po'.
Sal̲amat.

Drills

M̲eron silang langka'.
Wala' po' kaming pakwan.
Pabili nga' po' ng mangga.
Hindi' maganda ang s̲aging na ito.
P̲angit ang pakwang ito.
Magk̲ano ang pinyang iyan?
Isang daan lang po'.
Magk̲ano ang isang k̲ilong s̲aging?
Sixty-five po'.
Wala' akong barya. Buong limang daan lang ang p̲era ko.
Di' b̲ale, may panukli' po' ako.
isang daan, isang l̲ibo, isang milyon

Lesson 9
Ang pa<u>mi</u>lya ko

Mia shows her friend Mike a photo album with a picture of her family.

A 01

Ang pa<u>mi</u>lya ko

The family my

My family

A 02

Ito ang picture ng pamilya ko.

This the picture of family my.

This is the picture of my family.

A 03

Sino ito?

Who this?

Who is this?

A 04

Ito si Kuya Ryan.

This [Ang marker] Older Brother Ryan.

This is my older brother, Ryan.

Kuya means *older brother*. It can also be used to refer to other older male people, usually those belonging to the same generation as the speaker.

Ate is the female counterpart of **kuya**.

A 05

Ilang taon na siya?

How many-[linker] year now he/she?

How old is he?

A 06

Twenty-six na siya.

Twenty-six now he/she.

He's twenty-six.

A 07

May asawa na ba siya?

Has spouse now [question] he/she?

Is he married?

> **May asawa na** – *has a spouse, is married.*

A 08

M<u>e</u>ron. At may isang anak sila.

Has one. And have one-[linker] son/daughter they.

Yes. And they have one child.

Anak – *child (son or daughter).*

Bata' – *child (boy or girl).*

A 09

A. E ito? Siya ba ang <u>t</u>atay mo?

Ah. How about this? He/she [question] the dad your?

I see. How about this (one)? Is he your dad?

Here, **e** means *how about.*

A 10

<u>O</u>o. Den<u>ti</u>sta siya.

Yes. Dentist he/she.

Yes. He's a dentist.

A 11

Ano ang pangalan ng mga magulang mo?

What the name of [plural] parent your?

What are your parents' names?

A 12

Edwin at Arlene.

Edwin and Arlene.

Edwin and Arlene.

Edwin – *(the name) Edwin.*

Si Edwin – *(the person) Edwin.*

Sina Edwin at Arlene – *(the persons) Edwin and Arlene.*

A 13

At ito ang bunso', di ba?

And this the youngest child, right?

And this is the youngest, right?

Bunso' – *the youngest among siblings.*

A 14

Oo, si Julius. Nag-aaral pa siya.

Yes, [Ang marker] Julius. Is studying still he/she.

Yes, (that's) Julius. He's still studying.

Nag-aaral is a verb in the uncompleted form. This form is used when the action has been started but not completed, or when the action is habitual or is a general fact. We'll have a closer look at the verbs in later lessons.

Optional reading: Verb aspects: Overview (ETG p. 206/185).

Drills

B 01

Ilan ang kapatid mo?

How many the sibling your?

How many siblings do you have? (How many are your siblings?)

B 02

Dalawa.

Two.

Two.

B 03

Lalaki o babae ba ang mga kapatid mo?

Male or female [question] the [plural] sibling your?

Are they brothers or sisters? (Are your siblings male or female?)

B 04

Isang la<u>la</u>ki at isang ba<u>ba</u>e.

One-[linker] male and one-[linker] female.

One brother and one sister. (One male sibling and one female sibling.)

B 05

Emple<u>ya</u>do ba ang <u>ta</u>tay mo?

Employee [question] the dad your?

Is your dad an employee?

B 06

Hindi' siya emple<u>ya</u>do. <u>Me</u>ron siyang sa<u>ri</u>ling <u>kli</u>nik.

Not he/she employee. Has he/she-[linker] own-[linker] clinic.

He's not an employee. He has his own clinic.

Na/-ng is inserted after **siya**, which is enclitic.

B 07

M̱eron nang sar̲iling kl̲inik si Edwin.

Has now-[linker] own-[linker] clinic [Ang marker] Edwin.

Edwin has his own clinic now.

M̱erong sar̲iling kl̲inik becomes M̱eron nang sar̲iling kl̲inik, when **na** is added to the sentence. **Na/-ng** is inserted after **na** since **na** is enclitic.

B 08

May sar̲iling kl̲inik si Edwin.

Has own-[linker] clinic [Ang marker] Edwin.

Edwin has his own clinic.

B 09

Hindi' doktor si Arlene. Nurse siya.

Not doctor [Ang marker] Arlene. Nurse he/she.

Arlene is not a doctor. She's a nurse.

B 10

Nurse si Arlene. Dentista ang asawa niya.

Nurse [Ang marker] Arlene. Dentist the spouse his/her.

Arlene is a nurse. Her husband is a dentist.

B 11

Hindi' ako turista. Dito ako nakatira.

Not I tourist. Here I living.

I'm not a tourist. I live here.

Nakatira means *living (in a place)*.

Ako is enclitic.

Ang pamilya ko

Ito ang picture ng pamilya ko.
Sino ito?
Ito si Kuya Ryan.
Ilang taon na siya?
Twenty-six na siya.
May asawa na ba siya?
Meron. At may isang anak sila.
A. E ito? Siya ba ang tatay mo?
Oo. Dentista siya.
Ano ang pangalan ng mga magulang mo?
Edwin at Arlene.
At ito ang bunso', di ba?
Oo, si Julius. Nag-aaral pa siya.

Drills

Ilan ang kapatid mo?
Dalawa.
Lalaki o babae ba ang mga kapatid mo?
Isang lalaki at isang babae.
Empleyado ba ang tatay mo?
Hindi' siya empleyado. Meron siyang sariling klinik.
Meron nang sariling klinik si Edwin.
May sariling klinik si Edwin.
Hindi' doktor si Arlene. Nurse siya.
Nurse si Arlene. Dentista ang asawa niya.
Hindi' ako turista. Dito ako nakatira.

Lesson 10
Alas <u>kwa</u>tro na

Two friends are waiting for other friends to arrive.

A 01

Alas <u>kwa</u>tro na

Four o'clock now

It's four o'clock

Alas <u>kwa</u>tro – *four o'clock* or *at four o'clock.*

Alas <u>kwa</u>tro na. – *It's four o'clock.*

A 02

Alas kwatro na pero wala' pa sila dito.

Four o'clock | *now* | *but* | *are not* | *still* | *they* | *here.*

It's four o'clock, but they're still not here.

It is common to tell the time in Spanish and in English. **Alas kwatro na. / Four o'clock na.** – *It's four o'clock.*

A 03

Oo nga'. Pero sabi nila, darating sila.

Yes | *indeed.* | *But* | *said* | *by them,* | *will arrive* | *they.*

Yes (that's true). But they said they would come.

Sabi ko – *I said.*

Sabi mo – *you said.*

A 04

Sigurado ka?

Certain | *you?*

Are you sure?

A 05

Oo, tumawag ako kahapon.

Yes, called I yesterday.

Yes, I called yesterday.

Here, the verb **tumawag** is in the completed form.

Tumawag ako. – *I called.* **Tumawag na ako.** – *I have called; I had called (when something happened).*

A 06

Ganoon ba?

Like that (over there) [question]?

Is that so?

A 07

Teka. Tatawag ako uli'.

Wait. Will call I again.

Wait. I'll call (them) again.

Tatawag is the unstarted form of the verb **tumawag**.

Tatawag can be translated as *will call, calls (e.g. tomorrow)* or *is calling (e.g. tomorrow)*.

A 08

Sige.

OK.

OK.

A 09

Hello? Nasaan na kayo?

Hello? Where are now you (plural)?

Hello? Where are you?

A 10

Ano raw?

What they say?

What did they say?

Daw or **raw** – *he/she/they say, he/she/they said, I've heard, from what I hear.*

A 11

Akala' nila bukas ang appointment natin!

Thought (mistakenly) by them tomorrow the appointment our (incl. you)!

They thought our appointment was tomorrow!

Akala' ko – *I thought (mistakenly).*

Akala' mo – *you thought (mistakenly).*

Akala' nila introduces a clause here (a sentence within a sentence): **Bukas ang appointment natin.**

Enclitic words inside a clause follow the word order rules within the clause. Example: **Akala' nila, [meron akong kotse].** – *They thought I had a car.* Since **ako** is enclitic, it comes second in the clause **meron akong kotse**.

Optional reading: Enclitic words in clauses (ETG p. 342/308).

Drills

B 01

Anong oras na?

What-[linker] time now?

What time is it?

B 02

Ala una ng hapon.

One o'clock of afternoon.

One o'clock in the afternoon.

B 03

Alas dos ng umaga.

Two o'clock of morning.

Two o'clock in the morning.

B 04

Alas tres ang meeting namin.

At three o'clock the meeting our (excl. you).

Our meeting is at three o'clock.

B 05

Alas kwatro ang klase natin.

At four o'clock the class our (incl. you).

Our class is at four o'clock.

B 06

Alas singko na!

Five o'clock now!

It's (already) five o'clock!

B 07

Alas sais siguro.

At six o'clock maybe.

At six o'clock, maybe.

B 08

Alas syete yata'.

At seven o'clock I think.

At seven o'clock, I think.

B 09

Alas otso y medya.

Eight o'clock and a half.

Eight thirty.

B 10

Alas nwebe ng gabi.

Nine o'clock of evening/night.

Nine in the evening.

B 11

Alas dyes pa lang. Maaga pa.

Ten o'clock only. Early still.

It's only ten o'clock. It's still early.

Pa lang – *only, just.*

B 12

Alas onse ng gabi.

Eleven o'clock of evening/night.

Eleven in the evening.

B 13

Alas dose ng tanghali'.

Twelve o'clock of noon.

Twelve noon.

Optional reading: Parts of the day (ETG p. 301/271) and Clock time (ETG p. 302/271).

Before moving on to Lesson 11, it's a good idea to review Lessons 1–5. A quick and effective way to review previous lessons is to listen to the recordings while reading the lesson overview.

Alas kwatro na

Alas kwatro na pero wala' pa sila dito.
Oo nga'. Pero sabi nila, darating sila.
Sigurado ka?
Oo, tumawag ako kahapon.
Ganoon ba?
Teka. Tatawag ako uli'.
Sige.
Hello? Nasaan na kayo?
Ano raw?
Akala' nila bukas ang appointment natin!

Drills

Anong oras na?
Ala una ng hapon.
Alas dos ng umaga.
Alas tres ang meeting namin.
Alas kwatro ang klase natin.
Alas singko na!
Alas sais siguro.
Alas syete yata'.
Alas otso y medya.
Alas nwebe ng gabi.
Alas dyes pa lang. Maaga pa.
Alas onse ng gabi.
Alas dose ng tanghali'.

Lesson 11
Sa <u>sa</u>la

Julius asks his sister Mia what she's watching on TV.

A 01

Sa sala

In living room

In the living room

Sa is a Sa marker.

A 02

Ano iyan, Ate?

What that (near you), Older Sister?

What's that, Ate?

Ate means *older sister*. It can also be used to refer to other older female people, usually those belonging to the same generation as the speaker. The male counterpart of **ate** is **kuya**.

A 03

Bagong palabas.

New-[linker] show.

A new show.

A 04

Sino ang host?

Who the host?

Who's the host?

A 05

Hindi' ko alam. Bago rin siya.

Not by me known. New also he/she.

I don't know. He's also new.

A 06

Maganda ba ang palabas na iyan?

Nice [question] the program [linker] that (near you)?

Is that/the program nice?

> **Maganda** can mean *beautiful, nice* or *good*.

A 07

OK lang. Nakakatawa.

OK only. Funny.

It's OK. It's funny.

> **Nakaka-** – *causing* or *producing*.
>
> **Tawa** – *laughter*.
>
> **Nakakatawa** – *funny (causing laughter)*.

A 08

Gutom na ako. May tsokolate ba sa kusina?

Hungry now I. There is chocolate [question] in kitchen?

I'm hungry. Is there chocolate in the kitchen?

The sound /ts/ can be pronounced as /ch/.

A 09

Meron.

There is some.

Yes (there is).

A 10

Gusto mo ba ng tsokolate?

Wanted by you [question] [Ng marker] chocolate?

Would you like some chocolate? (Do you want some chocolate?)

Gusto mo ng (…). – *You want a/some (…).*

Gusto ko ng (…). – *I want a/some (…).*

A 11

Ayoko. Mamaya' na lang.

I don't want. Later today instead.

No, I don't want any. Maybe later.

Ayoko is short for **ayaw ko**, which means *I don't want/like (it)*.

Ayaw mo ng (…). – *You don't want a/any (…).*

Ayoko ng (…). – *I don't want a/any (…).*

A 12

Anong oras darating si Nanay?

What-[linker] time will arrive [Ang marker] Mom?

What time will mom arrive?

A 13

Alas sais yata'.

At six o'clock maybe.

At six, I guess.

Yata' expresses uncertainty. **Yata'** is enclitic, but **alas sais** cannot be separated.

Drills

B 01

Nakakatawa ang palabas.

Funny the show.

The show is funny.

B 02

Anong oras darating ang bisita mo?

What-[linker] time will arrive the guest your?

What time will your guest arrive?

B 03

Gusto mo ba ng saging?

Wanted by you [question] [Ng marker] banana?

Do you want a banana?

B 04

Ayoko. Busog na ako.

I don't want. Full now I.

No, I don't want any. I'm full.

Busog – *full (having eaten enough).*

B 05

Gusto mo ba ang sapatos na iyan?

Liked by you [question] the shoes [linker] that (near you)?

Do you like those shoes?

Gusto mo ang (…). – *You like/want the (…).*

Gusto ko ang (…). – *I like/want the (…).*

B 06

Oo, gusto ko ang sapatos na ito.

Yes, liked by me the shoes [linker] this.

Yes, I like these shoes.

B 07

Gusto mo ba ang rubber shoes na iyan?

Liked by you [question] the sports shoes [linker] that (near you)?

Do you like those sports shoes?

Rubber shoes – *sports shoes.*

B 08

Hindi', ang pangit e.

No, very ugly you see.

No, they're so ugly.

Ang is used as an intensifier here.

B 09

Ayaw niya ang rubber shoes na iyon.

Not liked by him/her the sports shoes [linker] that (over there).

He/she doesn't like those sports shoes.

The doer of **ayaw** is expressed as a Ng phrase (for example, **niya**).

Ang rubber shoes na iyon – *those sports shoes (over there).*

B 10

Anong kulay ang gusto mo?

What-[linker] color the liked by you?

What color do you like?

> **Ang gusto mo** – *the one(s) you like/want.*

B 11

Itim.

Black.

Black.

> Other common colors are: **puti'** – *white,* **dilaw** – *yellow,* **berde/green** – *green,* **asul/blue** – *blue,* **pula** – *red.*

Sa sala

Ano iyan, Ate?
Bagong palabas.
Sino ang host?
Hindi' ko alam. Bago rin siya.
Maganda ba ang palabas na iyan?
OK lang. Nakakatawa.
Gutom na ako. May tsokolate ba sa kusina?
Meron.
Gusto mo ba ng tsokolate?
Ayoko. Mamaya' na lang.
Anong oras darating si Nanay?
Alas sais yata'.

Drills

Nakakatawa ang palabas.
Anong oras darating ang bisita mo?
Gusto mo ba ng saging?
Ayoko. Busog na ako.
Gusto mo ba ang sapatos na iyan?
Oo, gusto ko ang sapatos na ito.
Gusto mo ba ang rubber shoes na iyan?
Hindi', ang pangit e.
Ayaw niya ang rubber shoes na iyon.
Anong kulay ang gusto mo?
Itim.

Lesson 12
Ang bi<u>si</u>ta

Mike is visiting Mia.

A 01

Ang bi<u>si</u>ta

The guest

The guest

A 02

Tao po'!

Person [polite]!

Hello! Anyone home?

A 03

Sino po' sila?

Who [polite] you (very polite)?

Who's there? (Who are you?) (polite)

Sila *(they)* is often used to address customers and high-ranking officials. It can also be used when asking an adult stranger who he or she is.

A 04

Si Michael Ramirez po' ito.

[Ang marker] Michael Ramirez [polite] this.

It's Michael Ramirez. (polite)

A 05

A, ikaw lang pala, Mike. Tuloy ka!

Ah, you just [surprise], Mike. Come in!

Oh, it's you, Mike. Come in!

Here, **pala** is used to express mild surprise at new or unexpected information.

Tuloy (ka/kayo). – *Come in.* Some verb roots, such as **tuloy**, can be used as a command, either alone or in combination with **ka/kayo**.

A 06

Hello Mia. Ang laki ng bahay niyo, a!

Hello Mia. How large of house your (plural), [admiration]!

Hello Mia. You (guys) have such a big house!

A at the end of a sentence can be used to express that you are surprised or impressed by something.

A 07

Hindi' naman. Saan ka galing?

No [softener]. Where you coming from?

Not really. Where did you just come from?

> Here, **naman** is used to soften what is said, or to make it less direct or less definite.

A 08

**Diyan lang.
Meron pala akong dala para sa iyo.**

*There (near you) just.
Have by the way I-[linker] something brought for you.*

Just there (nowhere in particular). By the way, I have/brought something for you.

> **Diyan lang** is a way to say *nowhere in particular*.
>
> **Merong dala** – *has brought something* (lit. has "something brought" or *has a "brought thing"*).
>
> **Pala** here means *by the way*.
>
> **Iyo** is a Sa pronoun.

A 09

Ang ganda ng bulaklak na ito! Salamat.

How beautiful of flower [linker] this! Thanks.

What a beautiful flower! Thanks.

A 10

Walang anuman.

There is no-[linker] anything.

You're welcome.

Walang anuman or, more informally, **wala' 'yon** means *you're welcome*.

A 11

Gusto mo bang uminom ng Coke?

Wanted by you [question]-[linker] to drink [Ng marker] Coke?

Do you want to drink Coke?

Uminom is a verb in the basic form.

Gusto mo -ng + basic form. – *You want to (...)*.

Gusto ko -ng + basic form. – *I want to (...)*.

Coke, the object of the action, is preceded by a Ng marker.

A 12

O sige.

OK.

OK.

Drills

B 01

Saan galing si Mike?

Where coming from [Ang marker] Mike?

Where is Mike coming from?

B 02

Ang ganda ng bahay nila!

How beautiful of house their!

Their house is so beautiful!

B 03

Kanino ito?

Whose this?

Whose is this?

> Here, **kanino** means *whose*.

B 04

Kay Alfred iyan.

Alfred's that (near you).

That's Alfred's.

Kay Alfred – *Alfred's.* Here **kay** indicates possession. Another example: **Sa bata' ang bag** – *The bag belongs to the child.*

B 05

Para kanino ito?

For whom this?

Who is this for?

Para kanino? – *For whom?*

B 06

Para kay Reybert iyan.

For Reybert that (near you).

That's for Reybert.

Para kay – *for* (for personal names).

B 07

<u>Pa</u>ra saan ang mga bulaklak na ito?

For what the [plural] flower [linker] this?

What are these flowers for?

<u>Pa</u>ra saan – *what for* or *for what purpose.*

B 08

<u>Pa</u>ra sa kasal <u>ma</u>maya'.

For wedding later today.

For the wedding later today.

B 09

<u>Ga</u>ling kay Mike ang mga bulaklak na iyan.

From Mike the [plural] flower [linker] that (near you).

Those flowers came from Mike.

<u>Ga</u>ling (sa/kay) – *from, coming from.*

Lesson 12   151

B 10

Ano ang meron doon sa Joe's Store?

What the there are over there at Joe's Store?

What do they have at Joe's Store?

Ang meron (doon) – *the thing(s) that are (there), the thing(s) they have (there), or the thing(s) happening (there).*

B 11

May mga libro at iba't ibang school supplies.

There are [plural] book and various-[linker] school supplies.

There are books and various school supplies.

Iba't iba – *various.*

Ang bisita

Tao po'!
Sino po' sila?
Si Michael Ramirez po' ito.
A, ikaw lang pala, Mike. Tuloy ka!
Hello Mia. Ang laki ng bahay niyo, a!
Hindi' naman. Saan ka galing?
Diyan lang. Meron pala akong dala para sa iyo.
Ang ganda ng bulaklak na ito! Salamat.
Walang anuman.
Gusto mo bang uminom ng Coke?
O sige.

Drills

Saan galing si Mike?
Ang ganda ng bahay nila!
Kanino ito?
Kay Alfred iyan.
Para kanino ito?
Para kay Reybert iyan.
Para saan ang mga bulaklak na ito?
Para sa kasal mamaya'.
Galing kay Mike ang mga bulaklak na iyan.
Ano ang meron doon sa Joe's Store?
May mga libro at iba't ibang school supplies.

Lesson 13
May tawag sa telepono

Dr. Molina is calling Dr. Gomez to say he won't play tennis on Sunday.

A 01

May tawag sa telepono

There is call on telephone

There's a phone call

A 02

Hello.

Hello.

Hello.

A 03

Hello, pwede pong makausap si Dr. Gomez?

Hello, could [polite]-[linker] be spoken to [Ang marker] Dr. Gomez?

Hello, could I speak to Dr. Gomez, please? (Could Dr. Gomez be spoken to?)

Makausap is a verb in the basic form.

Pwede -ng + basic form. – *can/could (…)* or *may/might (…) (expressing possibility or permission)*.

A 04

Sino po' sila?

Who [polite] you (very polite)?

May I know who's on the line? (Who are you?) (polite)

A 05

Si Dr. Molina ito.

[Ang marker] Dr. Molina this.

This is Dr. Molina.

A 06

Nasa klinik pa po' siya.

Is at clinic still [polite] he/she.

He's still at the clinic. (polite)

A 07

Oo nga' pala. Kailan siya babalik?

Yes, indeed after all. When he/she will return?

Oh yes, that's right (I'd forgotten about that). When will he be back?

A 08

Alas otso po' siguro.

At eight o'clock [polite] maybe.

At eight, I think. (polite)

A 09

A, pakisabi na lang sa kanya, hindi' ako pwedeng mag-tennis sa Linggo.

Ah, could you say just to him/her, not I can-[linker] play tennis on Sunday.

Ah (I see), well, just tell him I won't be able to play tennis on Sunday.

In **pakisabi**, **paki-** means *could you* (for requests).

The root of **pakisabi** is **sabi**, which, by itself, means *said* or *something said*.

A 10

Sige po'.

OK [polite].

I will. (polite)

Here, **sige po'** is a polite affirmative answer to a request, so you could translate it as *I will*.

A 11

Salamat.

Thanks.

Thanks.

158 Learning Tagalog: Fluency Made Fast and Easy

Drills

B 01

Pwede pong makausap si Mrs. Reyes?

Could [polite]-[linker] be spoken to [Ang marker] Mrs. Reyes?

Could I speak to Mrs. Reyes, please?

B 02

Sandali' lang.

Moment just.

Just a minute.

B 03

Kailan babalik si Tina?

When will return [Ang marker] Tina?

When will Tina return?

B 04

Pakisabi sa kanya, tumawag ako.

Could you say to *him/her,* called *I.*

Could you tell him/her that I called.

Tumawag is made up of the root **tawag** and the affix **-um-**.

Tawag, by itself, means *call (noun)* or *term (a word or expression)*.

Verbs with the affix **-um-** are called -um- verbs.

B 05

Hindi' ako pwedeng sumama sa Lunes.

Not I *can-[linker]* come along *on* Monday.

I can't come along on Monday.

Sumama is also an -um- verb.

For -um- verbs, the basic form and the completed form are identical.
Pwede akong su**ma**ma. (basic form) – *I can come along.*
Su**ma**ma ako. (completed form) – *I came along.*

B 06

Pupunta ka ba sa Maynila' sa Martes?

Will go you [question] to Manila on Tuesday?

Will you go to Manila on Tuesday?

B 07

Hindi'. Pumunta na ako noong Miyerkules.

No. Went already I last Wednesday.

No. I already went (there) last Wednesday.

> **Noong** indicates past time. **Noong Lunes** – *last Monday,* **noong January** – *last January,* **noong 1977 ("nineteen seventy-seven")** – *in 1977.*

B 08

Ano ang petsa sa Huwebes?

What the date on Thursday?

What's the date Thursday?

B 09

Ano ang meron sa Biyernes?

What the there is on Friday?

What's happening on Friday?

Ang meron (sa Biyernes) – *the thing(s) happening (on Friday).*

B 10

May lakad kami sa Sabado.

Have errand/outing we (excl. you) on Saturday.

We will go somewhere on Saturday. (We have an errand/outing on Saturday.)

Here, **lakad** means *errand* or *outing*.

B 11

Nasa simbahan sila tuwing Linggo mula' alas nwebe hanggang alas onse.

Are in church they every Sunday from nine o'clock until eleven o'clock.

They're in church every Sunday from nine till eleven.

May tawag sa telepono

Hello.
Hello, pwede pong makausap si Dr. Gomez?
Sino po' sila?
Si Dr. Molina ito.
Nasa klinik pa po' siya.
Oo nga' pala. Kailan siya babalik?
Alas otso po' siguro.
A, pakisabi na lang sa kanya, hindi' ako pwedeng mag-tennis sa Linggo.
Sige po'.
Salamat.

Drills

Pwede pong makausap si Mrs. Reyes?
Sandali' lang.
Kailan babalik si Tina?
Pakisabi sa kanya, tumawag ako.
Hindi' ako pwedeng sumama sa Lunes.
Pupunta ka ba sa Maynila' sa Martes?
Hindi'. Pumunta na ako noong Miyerkules.
Ano ang petsa sa Huwebes?
Ano ang meron sa Biyernes?
May lakad kami sa Sabado.
Nasa simbahan sila tuwing Linggo mula' alas nwebe hanggang alas onse.

Lesson 14
Tanghal<u>i</u>an sa restaurant

A man and his wife are having lunch at a restaurant, while their kids are staying with Grandma.

A 01

Tanghal<u>i</u>an sa restaurant

Lunch at restaurant

Lunch at the restaurant

Tang<u>h</u>ali' – *noon.* **Tanghal<u>i</u>an** – *lunch.*

A 02

Mabuti at na kay Lola ang mga bata'.

It's good that are with Grandma the [plural] child.

It's good that the kids are with Grandma.

Na kay – *is with (someone), is in (someone's) possession.* **Na kay Lola ang susi'.** – *Lola has the key. (The key is with Lola.)*

A 03

Bakit?

Why?

Why?

A 04

Mas tahimik at romantiko ang tanghalian natin, sweetheart.

More quiet and romantic the lunch our (incl. you), sweetheart.

(So) we can have a more quiet and romantic lunch, honey.

A 05

Oo nga'.

Yes indeed.

Yes, that's true.

A 06

Sige, ano ang order mo?

All right, what the order your?

All right, what are you having? (What's your order?)

A 07

Sopas lang. Hindi' ako masyadong gutom.

Soup only. Not I too-[linker] hungry.

Just soup. I'm not that hungry.

Masyado -ng (gutom) – *too (hungry)*.

Hindi' masyado -ng (gutom) – *not so (hungry)* or *not that (hungry)*.

A 08

Talaga? Ba<u>ha</u>la' ka.

Really? In charge you.

Really? It's up to you. (You're in charge.)

Here, **ba<u>ha</u>la'** means *in charge* or *responsible*.

A 09

Ikaw, ano ang order mo?

You, what the order your?

And you, what are you having?

A 10

Mukhang masarap ang litson na ito...

Looks tasty the roast pork [linker] this...

This roast pork looks good...

Mukha -ng – *looks, looks like (a/an), seems, it seems.* **Mukhang itlog** – *looks like an egg.*

A 11

O sige, isang sopas para sa akin
at isang litson para sa iyo...

*All right then, one-[linker] soup for me
and one-[linker] roast pork for you...*

All right then, one soup for me and one roast pork for you...

A 12

At pritong manok, inihaw na bangus, sinigang
at ice cream. Iyon lang.

*And fried-[linker] chicken, grilled [linker] milkfish, sinigang
and ice cream. That (over there) only.*

And fried chicken, grilled milkfish, sinigang and ice cream. That's all.

Sinigang is a kind of meat or fish stew with tamarind.

Drills

B 01

Mukhang malungkot si Lolo.

Looks sad [Ang marker] Lolo.

Lolo looks sad.

B 02

Bakit ang tahimik mo?

Why very quiet of you?

Why are you so quiet?

B 03

Malakas kumain ang lalaki.

Strong to eat the man.

The man is a big eater. (The man eats "strongly.")

Here, the adjective **(malakas)** preceding the basic form **(kumain)** expresses the way the action is characteristically performed by someone.

Optional reading: Adjective + basic form (characteristically performed) (ETG p. 230/207).

B 04

Para kanino ang isang buong manok na ito?

For *whom* the *one-[linker]* *whole-[linker]* *chicken* [linker] *this?*

Who is this whole chicken for?

B 05

Para sa kanya.

For *him/her.*

For him/her.

B 06

Wala' bang pagkain para sa atin?

There is no *[question]-[linker]* *food* *for* *us (incl. you)?*

Isn't there any food for us?

B 07

Sardinas lang ang para sa inyo.

Sardines only the for you (plural).

There are only sardines for you. (The ones for you are sardines only.)

Para sa inyo – *for you (plural).* **Ang para sa inyo** – *the one(s) for you (plural).*

B 08

Walang problema para sa amin.

There is no-[linker] problem for us (excl. you).

That's not a problem for us. (We don't mind.)

B 09

Meron pa bang pansit para sa kanila?

There is still [question]-[linker] pansit for them?

Is there still some pansit left for them?

Pansit is a noodle dish.

B 10

Wala', pero may adobo kung gusto nila.

There is none, but there is adobo if wanted by them.

There's none left, but there's adobo if they want some.

Kung – *if, when.*

B 11

Kanino iyan?

Whose that (near you)?

Whose is that?

B 12

Akin iyan!

Mine that (near you)!

That's mine!

Here, **akin** means *mine*. **(Sa) kanya iyan** – *That's his/hers*.

Optional reading: Sa pronouns (use #1) (ETG p. 66/57).

Tanghalian sa restaurant

Mabuti at na kay Lola ang mga bata'.
Bakit?
Mas tahimik at romantiko ang tanghalian natin, sweetheart.
Oo nga'.
Sige, ano ang order mo?
Sopas lang. Hindi' ako masyadong gutom.
Talaga? Bahala' ka.
Ikaw, ano ang order mo?
Mukhang masarap ang litson na ito…
O sige, isang sopas para sa akin at isang litson para sa iyo…
At pritong manok, inihaw na bangus, sinigang at ice cream. Iyon lang.

Drills

Mukhang malungkot si Lolo.
Bakit ang tahimik mo?
Malakas kumain ang lalaki.
Para kanino ang isang buong manok na ito?
Para sa kanya.
Wala' bang pagkain para sa atin?
Sardinas lang ang para sa inyo.
Walang problema para sa amin.
Meron pa bang pansit para sa kanila?
Wala', pero may adobo kung gusto nila.
Kanino iyan?
Akin iyan!

Lesson 15
Sa parlor

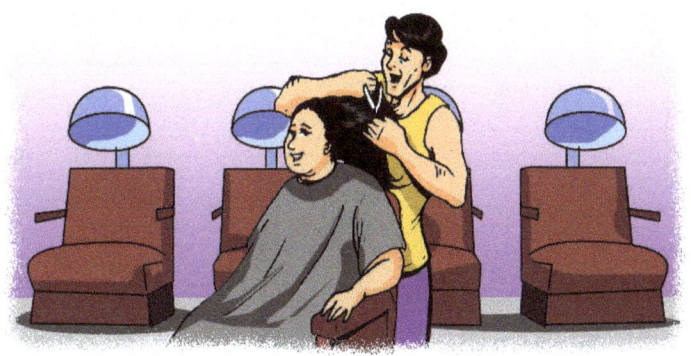

At the beauty parlor.

A 01

Sa parlor

At beauty parlor

At the beauty parlor

Parlor means *beauty parlor* or *hairdresser* in the Philippines.

A 02

Ano pong style ang gusto ninyo, ma'am?

What [polite]-[linker] style the wanted by you (polite), ma'am?

What style would you like, ma'am?

> **Gusto ninyo** – *you (plural) want/like/would like.* **Ang gusto ninyo** – *the one that you (plural) want/like/would like.*

A 03

Parang itong style sa picture na ito.

Like this-[linker] style on picture [linker] this.

Like the style on this picture.

> You can also say **itong style na ito sa picture na ito**. In such phrases as **itong style na ito**, the second **ito/iyan/iyon** may be dropped when more information about the noun is given right after it. In this case, the additional information given about **style** is **sa picture na ito** – *on this picture*.
>
> Here, **para -ng** means *like*.

A 04

Ganito po'?

Like this [polite]?

Like this? (polite)

Ganito – *like this.*

Ganyan – *like that (near you).*

Ganoon – *like that (far from you and me).*

A 05

Oo, ganyan. Gusto ko, maigsi' sa harap at mahaba' sa likod.

Yes, like that (near you). Wanted by me, short in front and long in back.

Yes, like that. I want it short in front and long at the back.

Gusto ko – *I want/like/would like.*

A 06

Sige po'. [...]

All right [polite]. [...]

All right. (polite) [...]

A 07

Narinig po' ba ninyo ang balita' kanina sa radyo?

Was heard [polite] [question] by you (polite) the news earlier today on radio?

Did you hear the news on the radio earlier today? (polite)

Narinig is the completed form of **marinig**. With **marinig**, the POD of the sentence is the object (what is heard; in this case, **ang balita'**) and the doer is expressed as a Ng phrase (in this case, **ninyo**). If the object of an action in a basic Tagalog sentence is definite, it generally becomes the POD of the sentence. In English, however, a definite object does not have to be the subject. This is one of the main differences between the Tagalog POD and the English subject.

Recommended reading: The Tagalog POD and the English subject (ETG p. 38/33).

A 08

Ano iyon?

What that (over there)?

What was that about?

Here, **iyon** refers to a thing or idea that is not closely identified with the speaker or the listener.

A 09

**May isang lalaki raw po' na nalaglag
sa eroplano kanina.**

*There is one-[linker] man they say [polite] [linker] fell
from airplane earlier today.*

They said there's a man that fell out of an airplane earlier today. (polite)

> Here, the linker **na** can be translated as *that*.

A 10

Talaga? Namatay ba siya?

Really? Died [question] he/she?

Really? Did he die?

A 11

**Hindi' po', buhay pa po'.
At wala' raw pong sugat.**

*No [polite], alive still [polite].
And has no they say [polite]-[linker] wound.*

No, he's still alive. And they said he's uninjured. (polite)

A 12

Impo_si_ble. K_we_ntong-bar_be_ro lang iyan!

Impossible. Barber's story just that (near you)!

That's impossible. That's just hearsay!

K_we_ntong-bar_be_ro – *hearsay, tall tale, urban legend.* **K_we_ntong-bar_be_ro** is a compound noun.

Optional reading: Compound nouns (ETG p. 99/86).

Drills

B 01

Mahaba' ang buhok niya.

Long the hair his/her.

He/she has long hair. (His/her hair is long.)

B 02

Maigsi' ang balahibo ng pusa'.

Short the fur of cat.

The cat has short fur. (The cat's fur is short.)

B 03

Parang ganito ba ang hitsura niya?

Somewhat like this [question] the appearance his/her?

Does/Did he/she look somewhat like this?

Parang ganito – *somewhat like this.*

There are a few words that enclitic words may, but do not have to, immediately follow. One of them is **para (-ng)**. For example, **Parang ganito ba?** and **Para bang ganito?** are both correct.

Optional reading: Exceptions to the follow-the-first-word-rule (#3) (ETG p. 344/309).

B 04

Oo, parang ganyan.

Yes, somewhat like that (near you).

Yes, somewhat like that.

B 05

Nagulat ako!

Was startled I!

I was startled!

Nagulat is the completed form of **magulat**. With **magulat**, the POD **(ako)** is the doer or "experiencer" of the action or emotion.

B 06

Nakakagulat ang kwento na iyan.

Startling the story [linker] that (near you).

That's a startling story. (That story is startling.)

Gulat – *surprise*. **Nakakagulat** – *startling*.

B 07

Nakakahiya' naman iyan!

Embarrassing [sympathy/shock/etc.] that (near you)!

That's so embarrassing!

Hiya' – *shame, embarrassment.* **Nakakahiya'** – *embarrassing.*

Naman may be used to express surprise, admiration, irritation, impatience, disgust, sympathy or other emotions.

B 08

Nakakainis ang aso na ito.

Annoying the dog [linker] this.

This dog is annoying.

Inis – *annoyance.* **Nakakainis** – *annoying.*

B 09

Na<u>g</u>hugas ka ba ng kamay, anak?

Washed you [question] [Ng marker] hand, son/daughter?

Did you wash your hands, sweetie?

In the expression **naghugas ng kamay**, **kamay** is understood to be plural and to be one's own hands.

Here **ng** introduces the object of the action.

Optional reading: Ng markers (use #3) (ETG p. 46/40).

B 10

<u>O</u>po', ma<u>l</u>inis ang mga kamay ko.

Yes (polite), clean the [plural] hand my.

Yes, my hands are clean.

So far, not much attention has been given to the verbs, in order to keep the lessons simple. After Lesson 20, the verbs will be covered more systematically.

Before moving on to Lesson 16, it's a good idea to review Lessons 6–10.

Sa parlor

Ano pong style ang gusto ninyo, ma'am?
Pa̱rang itong style sa picture na ito.
Ganito po'?
O̱o, ganyan. Gusto ko, maigsi' sa harap at maha̱ba' sa likod.
Sige po'. […]
Narinig po' ba ninyo ang bali̱ta' kani̱na sa ra̱dyo?
Ano iyon?
May isang lala̱ki raw po' na nalaglag sa eropla̱no kani̱na.
Talaga? Namatay ba siya?
Hindi' po', buhay pa po'. At wala' raw pong su̱gat.
Imposi̱ble. Kwe̱ntong-barbe̱ro lang iyan!

Drills

Maha̱ba' ang buhok niya.
Maigsi' ang balahi̱bo ng pu̱sa'.
Pa̱rang ganito ba ang hitsu̱ra niya?
O̱o, pa̱rang ganyan.
Nagu̱lat ako!
Naka̱kagulat ang kwe̱nto na iyan.
Naka̱kahiya' naman iyan!
Naka̱kainis ang a̱so na ito.
Naghu̱gas ka ba ng kamay, anak?
O̱po', mali̱nis ang mga kamay ko.

Lesson 16
Nan<u>di</u>to na sina <u>Ti</u>ta Amy

Tita Amy and Tito Juan have arrived in the Philippines.

A 01

Nan<u>di</u>to na sina <u>Ti</u>ta Amy

Are here now [Ang marker] Aunt Amy

Tita Amy and her husband have arrived

Sina is the plural form of **si**. **Sina <u>Ti</u>ta Amy** – *Tita Amy and company.*

A 02

Nandito na sina Tita Amy sa Pilipinas.

Are here now [Ang marker] Aunt Amy in Philippines.

Tita Amy and her husband/family are now in the Philippines.

A 03

Talaga? Kailan sila dumating?

Really? When they arrived?

Really? When did they arrive?

A 04

Noong Pebrero. Nasa Lipa sila ngayon.

Last February. Are in Lipa they now.

In February. They're in Lipa right now.

A 05

May bahay ba sila roon?

Have house [question] they over there?

Do they have a house there?

A 06

Oo. May bahay-bakasyunan sila roon. Matagal na.

Yes. Have vacation home they over there. Long (for time) now.

Yes. They have a vacation home there. (They've had it) for a long time now.

> **Matagal na** – *for a long time* or *long ago*.

A 07

Retired na ba si Tito Juan?

Retired now [question] [Ang marker] Uncle Juan?

Is Tito Juan retired now?

A 08

Oo, matanda' na siya.

Yes, old already he/she.

Yes, he's already old.

Lesson 16

A 09

**Magkikita' pala kami sa Biyernes.
Gusto mo bang sumama?**

*Will meet by the way we (excl. you) on Friday.
Wanted by you [question]-[linker] to come along?*

By the way, we'll see each other on Friday. Do you want to come along?

Pala, kami, mo and **ba** are enclitic.

A 10

Gaano katagal ang byahe mula' Calamba' hanggang Lipa?

How long (for time) the trip from Calamba to Lipa?

How long does it take to get from Calamba to Lipa? (How long is the trip from Calamba to Lipa?)

Gaano ka- + adjective root – *how big, fast etc.* **Gaano katagal** – *how long (for time).* **Gaano kalaki** – *how big.*

The affix **ka-** + adjective root can also be used after **ganito, ganyan** and **ganoon**, to mean *this/that big, fast etc.* (expressing similarity).

Optional reading: **ganito/ganyan/ganoon ka-** (ETG p. 285/256).

A 11

Dep__e__nde sa tr__a__pik. M__in__san mga dalawang __o__ras.

It depends on traffic. Sometimes about two-[linker] hour.

It depends on the traffic. Sometimes it can take about two hours.

Dep__e__nde – *it depends, depending on.*

Mga means *about* or *around* when used before a number or a time expression.

A 12

Ang l__a__yo' pala. Hindi' na lang ako sas__a__ma.

Very far after all. Not instead I will come along.

It's quite far after all. I'd rather not go then.

Here, **pala** means *after all*.

Na lang – instead of what has been said or planned before or what is expected.

A 13

Mar_a_mi silang dalang pasal_u_bong g_a_ling sa States.

Have many they-[linker] brought-[linker] gift from States.

They brought a lot of gifts from the States. (They have a lot of brought gifts from the States.)

Here, **mar_a_mi** means *have many* (…).

Dala – *brought, something brought.*

Pasal_u_bong – *gift brought by a returning traveler or a newly-arrived person.*

A 14

**Talaga? Dalawang _o_ras lang pala e!
Sige, sas_a_ma na ako!**

*Really? Two-[linker] hour only after all [relief]!
OK, will come along after all I!*

Really? So it's only two hours, eh! All right then, I'm coming along!

(…) lang pala e! – *So it's only (…), eh! (It's no big deal at all.)*

Na means *after all* here.

Drills

B 01

Enero, Pebrero, Marso

January, February, March

January, February, March

B 02

Abril, Mayo, Hunyo

April, May, June

April, May, June

B 03

Hulyo, Agosto, Setyembre

July, August, September

July, August, September

B 04

Oktubre, Nobyembre, Disyembre

October, November, December

October, November, December

B 05

Magkikita' kami sa Agosto.

Will meet we (excl. you) in August.

We'll see each other in August.

B 06

Isang oras lang ang byahe.

One-[linker] hour only the trip.

The trip takes only one hour.

B 07

Ayokong sumama.

I don't want-[linker] to come along.

I don't want to come along.

Ayaw ko -ng + basic form or **Ayoko -ng** + basic form – *I don't want/like to (…).*

B 08

May pasalubong kayo galing kina Tita Amy.

Have gift you (plural) from (plural) Aunt Amy.

You have a present(s) from Tita Amy and her husband/family.

Kina is the plural form of **kay**.

Nandito na sina Tita Amy

Nandito na sina Tita Amy sa Pilipinas.
Talaga? Kailan sila dumating?
Noong Pebrero. Nasa Lipa sila ngayon.
May bahay ba sila roon?
Oo. May bahay-bakasyunan sila roon. Matagal na.
Retired na ba si Tito Juan?
Oo, matanda' na siya.
Magkikita' pala kami sa Biyernes. Gusto mo bang sumama?
Gaano katagal ang byahe mula' Calamba' hanggang Lipa?
Depende sa trapik. Minsan mga dalawang oras.
Ang layo' pala. Hindi' na lang ako sasama.
Marami silang dalang pasalubong galing sa States.
Talaga? Dalawang oras lang pala e! Sige, sasama na ako!

Drills

Enero, Pebrero, Marso
Abril, Mayo, Hunyo
Hulyo, Agosto, Setyembre
Oktubre, Nobyembre, Disyembre
Magkikita' kami sa Agosto.
Isang oras lang ang byahe.
Ayokong sumama.
May pasalubong kayo galing kina Tita Amy.

Lesson 17
Sa hotel

Mr. de Leon checks in at the hotel lobby and asks where the nearest ATM is.

A 01

Sa hotel

At hotel

At the hotel

A 02

Ano pong pangalan nila?

What [polite]-[Ang marker] name your (very polite)?

May I have your name, sir? (What is your name, sir?)

Ang may sometimes be shortened to **-ng** (**po' ang** becomes **pong**).

Nila *(their)* is often used instead of **mo** *(your, singular)* when speaking to customers and high-ranking officials.

A 03

Tomas de Leon.

Tomas de Leon.

Tomas de Leon.

A 04

Hanggang kailan po' sila rito?

Until when [polite] you (very polite) here?

How long (till when) will you be staying here, sir?

A 05

Hanggang bukas ng umaga.

Until tomorrow of morning.

Until tomorrow morning.

Bukas ng umaga – *tomorrow morning.* **Bukas ng ala una** – *tomorrow at one o'clock.*

A 06

Aircon room po'?

Air-conditioned room [polite]?

Would you like an air-conditioned room, sir?

Aircon is the commonly-used abbreviation for *air conditioner* or *air-conditioned.*

A 07

Oo.

Yes.

Yes.

A 08

Sige po', eto po' ang susi'. Room number 7 po'.

OK [polite], here is [polite] the key. Room number 7 [polite].

OK, sir. Here is your key. It's room number 7, sir.

A 09

Nasa second floor. Nandoon po' ang elevator.

Is on second floor. Is over there [polite] the elevator.

It's on the second floor. The elevator is over there. (polite)

A 10

Salamat. Nasaan pala ang pinakamalapit na ATM dito?

Thanks. Where is by the way the nearest [linker] ATM here.

Thanks. By the way, where is the nearest ATM?

Pinaka- – *most (…)/-est.* **Malapit** – *near.* **Pinakamalapit** – *nearest.*

Pinakamaganda – *most beautiful, prettiest.*

A 11

Paglabas po' ninyo, kumanan po' kayo.

When going out [polite] your (polite), turn right [polite] you (polite).

When you go out, turn right. (polite)

Here, **pag-** + root means *when (...)*. This may be followed by a Ng marker or a Ng pronoun. **Paglabas ninyo** – *when you (plural) go out.*

Basic form + **ka/kayo** is one of the ways to give directions or a command. **Kumanan ka/kayo.** – *Turn right.*

A 12

Dumeretso po' kayo hanggang sa crossing.

Go straight [polite] you (polite) until intersection.

Go straight on until the intersection. (polite)

Dumeretso kayo. – *Go straight.*

Hanggang or **hanggang sa** – *until, up to, to.*

Crossing usually refers to the busiest intersection in town.

A 13

**T̲apos, kumaliwa' po' kayo.
May ba̲ngko po' roon.**

*Then, turn left [polite] you (polite).
There is bank [polite] over there.*

Then, turn left. There's a bank over there. (polite)

A 14

Sala̲mat.

Thanks.

Thanks.

Drills

B 01

Hanggang anong o̱ras bukas ang lobby?

Until what-[linker] time open the lobby?

Till what time is the lobby open?

B 02

Hanggang alas o̱nse po'.

Until eleven o'clock [polite].

Until eleven o'clock. (polite)

B 03

Twenty-four hours po' kaming bukas.

Twenty-four hours [polite] we (excl. you)-[linker] open.

We're open 24 hours. (polite)

> **Twenty-four hours na bukas** – open 24 hours. **Na/-ng** is inserted after **po'** and **kami**, which are both enclitic.

B 04

Bawal pumasok.

Prohibited to enter.

No entry.

Bawal + basic form – (…) is prohibited; It's prohibited to (…). **Bawal pumasok.** – It's prohibited to enter; Entering is prohibited; No entry.

B 05

Bawal lumusot.

Prohibited to pass (overtake).

Do not pass. (No overtaking.)

Lumusot – to pass (overtake), to go through a narrow place (such as a narrow opening).

B 06

Bawal umihi' dito.

Prohibited to urinate here.

No urinating here.

B 07

Bawal tumigil dito.

Prohibited to stop here.

No stopping here.

B 08

Bawal magtapon ng basura.

Prohibited to throw away [Ng marker] garbage.

No dumping of trash.

B 09

Mag-ingat. Madulas ang kalsada.

Take care. Slippery the road.

Caution. Slippery road.

The basic form, by itself, can also be used for giving commands or directions to the public.

B 10

kaliwa', kanan

left, right

left, right

Sa hotel

Ano pong pangalan nila?
Tomas de Leon.
Hanggang kailan po' sila rito?
Hanggang bukas ng umaga.
Aircon room po'?
Oo.
Sige po', eto po' ang susi'. Room number 7 po'.
Nasa second floor. Nandoon po' ang elevator.
Salamat. Nasaan pala ang pinakamalapit na ATM dito?
Paglabas po' ninyo, kumanan po' kayo.
Dumeretso po' kayo hanggang sa crossing.
Tapos, kumaliwa' po' kayo. May bangko po' roon.
Salamat.

Drills

Hanggang anong oras bukas ang lobby?
Hanggang alas onse po'.
Twenty-four hours po' kaming bukas.
Bawal pumasok.
Bawal lumusot.
Bawal umihi' dito.
Bawal tumigil dito.
Bawal magtapon ng basura.
Mag-ingat. Madulas ang kalsada.
kaliwa', kanan

Lesson 18
Ang init!

It's a very hot day and the air conditioner in the office doesn't work, or does it?

A 01

Ang init!

How hot!

It's so hot!

A 02

Grabe ang init dito!

Incredible the heat here!

It's so hot here! (The heat here is incredible!)

Grabe – *incredible, amazing. By itself, it means* Wow! *or* Oh my!

A 03

Oo. Sobrang init. Mas mainit pa rito kaysa sa labas.

Yes. So-[linker] hot. More hot even here than in outside.

Yes. It's so hot. It's even hotter here than outside.

Sobra -ng + adjective root – *so (...).* **Sobrang ganda** – *so pretty.* Used this way, **sobra -ng** is an adjective intensifier (like **ang** + root). What the adjective describes (if present) is expressed as a Ng phrase. **Sobrang init ng sopas!** – *The soup is so hot!*

Mas... pa – *even more (...) / even (...)-er.* **Mas mainit pa** – *even hotter.*

Mas... kaysa – *more (...) than / (...)-er than.*

A 04

Di ba bago ang aircon natin?

Isn't it new the air conditioner our (incl. you)?

Isn't our air conditioner new?

Di ba is used for confirming something. It may be translated as *isn't it/he/she, aren't they, didn't you, right?* etc. and may be used at the beginning or at the end of a sentence.

A 05

Oo.

Yes.

Yes.

A 06

Nakabukas ba ang aircon?

Turned on [question] the air conditioner?

Is the air conditioner turned on?

A 07

Oo, tingnan mo.

Yes, be looked at by you.

Yes, look (at the aircon).

Tingnan is a verb in the basic form. Its literal translation is *(to) be looked at*. The POD is the thing looked at, which is omitted here. This type of verb will be covered in detail later.

Basic form + **mo/ninyo** is one of the ways to give a command or directions. **Tingnan mo ang aircon.** – *Look at the aircon.*

A 08

Bakit parang mas malakas pa ang lumang aircon kaysa rito?

Why seems more strong even the old-[linker] air conditioner than this.

Why does the old air conditioner seem to be even stronger than this one?

Here, **para -ng** means *seems (to be/like)*.

Mas… (kaysa) + Sa phrase – *more (…)/-er than (…)*.

A 09

Baka naman may problema ito?

Maybe [contrast] has problem this?

Maybe there's a problem with this one?

> **Naman** can be used to show contrast with what usually happens, what has recently or just happened, or what might be expected.

A 10

Hindi', mukhang ayos naman.

No, seems in working order [contrast].

No, it seems to be working just fine.

> **Naman** can also be used to show contrast with what somebody said, for instance, when expressing an opposing opinion or correcting someone.

A 11

Teka. Naririnig mo ba ang mga sasakyan sa labas?

Wait. Can be heard by you [question] the [plural] vehicle in outside?

Wait. Can you hear the cars outside?

Naririnig is the uncompleted form of **marinig**. With **marinig**, the POD of the sentence is the object (what is heard; in this case, **ang mga sasakyan sa labas**) and the doer is expressed as a Ng phrase (in this case, **mo**). If the object of an action in a basic Tagalog sentence is definite, it generally becomes the POD of the sentence.

A 12

Oo, bakit?

Yes, why?

Yes, why?

A 13

Kasi bukas ang bintana' sa likod!

Because open the window at back!

That's because the window at the back is open!

Kasi – *because, that's because.* **Kasi** is enclitic, but can also be placed at the beginning of the sentence or clause (sentence within a sentence).

Drills

B 01

Mas ma_i_nit sa Mayn_i_la' kaysa sa Bag_ui_o.

More hot in Manila than in Baguio.

It's hotter in Manila than in Baguio.

B 02

Mas matangkad ka kaysa kay Ray.

More tall you than [Sa marker] Ray.

You're taller than Ray.

> **Mas** cannot be immediately followed by enclitic words, such as **ka**.

B 03

Mar_u_nong ka bang mag-chess?

Know how you [question]-[linker] to play chess?

Do you know how to play chess?

> **Mar_u_nong (-ng)** + basic form – *know how to (…)*. If the word preceding the basic form ends in a vowel or /n/, **-ng** may be added.

B 04

Oo, pero mas **magaling** ka **sa** chess **kaysa** sa **akin.**

Yes, but more good you at chess than [Sa marker] me.

Yes, but you're better at chess than me.

Magaling – *good (able to do something well).*

B 05

tagsibol, tag-init, tag-ulan, taglagas, taglamig

spring, hot season/summer, rainy season, autumn, cold season/winter

spring, hot season/summer, rainy season, autumn, cold season/winter

B 06

Malakas ang hangin at ulan.

Strong the wind and rain.

The wind is strong and it's raining hard. (The wind and rain are strong/heavy.)

B 07

Ang lakas ng bagyo!

How strong of typhoon!

The typhoon is so strong!

B 08

Nakakatakot ang kidlat.

Scary the lightning.

The lightning is scary.

Takot – *fear.* **Na**ka**ka**ta**kot** – *frightening, scary.*

B 09

Takot siya sa kidlat.

Afraid he/she of lightning.

He/she's afraid of lightning.

Takot (sa) – *scared (of), afraid (of).*

Ang i̱nit!

G̱rabe ang i̱nit ḏito!
O̱o. S̱obrang i̱nit. Mas ma̱init pa ṟito kaysa sa labas.
Di ba ḇago ang aircon ṉatin?
O̱o.
Nakabukas ba ang aircon?
O̱o, tingnan mo.
Ḇakit p̱arang mas malakas pa ang ḻumang aircon kaysa ṟito?
Baka naman may probḻema ito?
Hindi', mukhang ayos naman.
Ṯeka. Naṟirinig mo ba ang mga sasakyan sa labas?
O̱o, ḇakit?
Kasi bukas ang binṯana' sa likod!

Drills

Mas ma̱init sa Mayṉila' kaysa sa Ḇaguio.
Mas matangkad ka kaysa kay Ray.
Maṟunong ka bang mag-chess?
O̱o, p̱ero mas magaling ka sa chess kaysa sa a̱kin.
tagsibol, tag-init, tag-ulan, taglagas, taglamig
Malakas ang ẖangin at ulan.
Ang lakas ng bagyo!
Naḵakaṯakot ang kidlat.
Takot siya sa kidlat.

Lesson 18

Lesson 19
May sakit ang a<u>sa</u>wa ko

Maria talks to her colleague about her husband's stomach ache the previous night.

A 01

May sakit ang a<u>sa</u>wa ko

Has illness the spouse my

My husband is ill

A 02

Anong balita'?

What-[Ang marker] news?

How's it going? (What's the news?)

Here, **ang** is shortened to **-ng**. Ano ang balita? – Anong balita?

A 03

May sakit ang asawa ko. Mula' pa kagabi.

Has illness the spouse my. Since last night.

My husband is ill. Since last night.

Mula' pa – *since (as long ago as)*; used with a past time expression to imply that something has been the case since some time ago. The speaker feels it has been quite a long time.

A 04

Talaga?

Really?

Really?

A 05

Oo. Nagising siya noong hatinggabi.

Yes. Woke up he/she last midnight.

Yes. He woke up in the middle of the night (at midnight).

A 06

Sabi niya, masama' ang pakiramdam niya.

Said by him/her, bad the feeling his/her.

He said he wasn't feeling well.

A 07

Sabi ko, ano ang problema?

Said by me, what the problem?

I said, "What's wrong?"

A 08

Masakit daw ang tyan niya.

Painful he/she said the belly his/her.

He said his tummy hurt.

A 09

Tapos?

Then?

And then?

A 10

**Sabi ko sa kanya,
bakit hindi' ka uminom ng gamot?**

*Said by me to him/her,
why not you drink [Ng marker] medicine?*

I told him, "Why don't you take some medicine?"

Bakit hindi' ka + basic form – *why don't you (…)*.

A 11

Sabi niya, nakainom na raw siya.

Said by him/her, had been able to drink already he/she said he/she.

He said he already took some (medicine).

Nakainom *(was able to drink)* is the completed form of **makainom**. Here, the affix **maka-** means *to be able to*.

Nakainom na – *has/had been able to drink*.

A 12

'Yun pala, buong bote ang ininom niya!

It turns out, whole-[linker] bottle the was drunk by him/her!

It turns out he drank the whole bottle!

'Yun is short for **iyon**.

Ininom is a verb used as a noun here. It is the completed form of **inumin** (root is **inom**, affix is **-in**, POD is the object). More on this later!

Ang ininom niya – *the thing that was drunk by him/her.*

Optional reading: Verbs, adjectives etc. used as nouns (ETG p. 101/87).

Drills

B 01

Sabi niya, magaling na siya.

Said by him/her, well again now he/she.

He/she said he/she's well again.

> Here, **magaling na** means *no longer ill* or *well again (has recovered from illness)*.

B 02

May sipon ako.

Have cold I.

I have a cold.

B 03

May trangkaso ang pamangkin ko.

Has flu the nephew/niece my.

My nephew/niece has the flu.

B 04

Magaling ka na ba?

Well again you now [question]?

Are you feeling well again? (Have you recovered?)

Notice the order of the enclitic words: **ka na ba**.

B 05

Hindi', may ubo at lagnat pa ako.

No, have cough and fever still I.

No, I still have a cough and a fever.

B 06

May lagnat ka ba?

Have fever you [question]?

Do you have a fever?

B 07

Wala', pero nahihilo ako.

Have none, but am feeling dizzy I.

No, but I'm feeling dizzy.

B 08

Masama' ang pakiramdam ko.

Bad the feeling my.

I'm not feeling well.

B 09

Masakit ang ulo ko.

Painful the head my.

I have a headache.

B 10

Pumunta ka na ba sa doktor?

Went you already [question] to doctor?

Have you gone to a doctor?

Pumunta na – *has/had gone.*

Ka has a higher priority than **na**.

B 11

Hindi' pa.

Not yet.

Not yet.

Here, **pa** means *yet*.

May sakit ang asawa ko

Anong balita'?
May sakit ang asawa ko. Mula' pa kagabi.
Talaga?
Oo. Nagising siya noong hatinggabi.
Sabi niya, masama' ang pakiramdam niya.
Sabi ko, ano ang problema?
Masakit daw ang tyan niya.
Tapos?
Sabi ko sa kanya, bakit hindi' ka uminom ng gamot?
Sabi niya, nakainom na raw siya.
'Yun pala, buong bote ang ininom niya!

Drills

Sabi niya, magaling na siya.
May sipon ako.
May trangkaso ang pamangkin ko.
Magaling ka na ba?
Hindi', may ubo at lagnat pa ako.
May lagnat ka ba?
Wala', pero nahihilo ako.
Masama' ang pakiramdam ko.
Masakit ang ulo ko.
Pumunta ka na ba sa doktor?
Hindi' pa.

Lesson 20
Sa mall

Julius and Mia are shopping at a mall.

A 01

Sa mall

In mall

In the mall

A 02

Kailangan kong bumili ng tela.

Needed by me-[linker] to buy [Ng marker] cloth.

I need to buy some cloth.

Kailangan ko -ng + basic form – *I need to/ought to/must/should (…)*.

Kailangan often connotes a self-imposed need or duty.

A 03

Anong klaseng tela?

What-[linker] kind-[linker] cloth?

What kind of cloth?

Klaseng tela or **klase ng tela** – *kind of cloth*.

A 04

Katsa lang. Para sa project ko.

Muslin only. For project my.

Just muslin. It's for my project.

A 05

Ikaw, may bibilhin ka ba?

You, have will be bought you [question]?

And you? Do you have anything to buy?

Bibilhin *(will be bought)* is the unstarted form of the verb **bilhin** *(to be bought)*. Here, it is used as a noun. It means *thing that will be bought*.

May bibilhin ka. – *You have something that will be bought.* In natural English: *You will buy something* or *You have something to buy*.

The verbs will be covered in detail very soon.

A 06

Wala'. Ubos na kasi ang pera ko.

Have none. Used up already because the money my.

No, because I already spent all my money. (No, because my money is used up already.)

Na and **kasi** are enclitic.

A 07

Naglaro' kasi ako ng computer games kasama ng mga kaibigan ko.

Played because I [Ng marker] computer games together with [plural] friend my.

That's because I played computer games with my friends.

Kasama ng – *together with, along with.*

A 08

Kaya' pala. Ano ang gagawin mo?

So that's why. What the will be done by you?

Oh, so that's why. What will you do then?

Gagawin *(will be done)* is the unstarted form of **gawin** *(to be done)*. Here, it is used as a noun. **Ang gagawin** – *the thing that will be done.*

A 09

Tatambay na lang ako sa bookstore.

Will hang out just I at bookstore.

I'll just hang out at the bookstore.

A 10

N<u>a</u>saan pala si T<u>a</u>tay?

Where is by the way [Ang marker] Dad?

By the way, where's Dad?

A 11

N<u>a</u>sa k<u>o</u>tse siya. Nat<u>u</u>tulog sig<u>u</u>ro.

Is in car he/she. Is sleeping maybe.

He's in the car. I guess he's sleeping.

Mat<u>u</u>log – *to sleep.* **Nat<u>u</u>tulog** – *sleeps* or *is/was sleeping* (uncompleted form).

A 12

Sige, magk<u>i</u>ta' na lang t<u>a</u>yo m<u>a</u>maya' ha?

All right, meet just we (incl. you) later today, OK?

All right, we'll just meet later, OK? (Let's just meet later, OK?)

Here, **ha?** means *OK?*

Magk<u>i</u>ta' is a verb in the basic form.

Drills

B 01

Kai<u>la</u>ngan niyang bumili ng gamot.

Needed by him/her-[linker] to buy [Ng marker] medicine.

He/she needs to buy medicine.

> **Kai<u>la</u>ngan niya -ng** + basic form – *He/she needs to/ought to/must/should (...).*

B 02

Hindi' niya kai<u>la</u>ngang bumili ng pag<u>ka</u>in.

Not by him/her needed-[linker] to buy [Ng marker] food.

He/she doesn't need to buy food.

> Since **niya** is enclitic, it follows the first word of the sentence.

B 03

Mag<u>ka</u>no ang pama<u>sa</u>he hanggang sa mall?

How much the fare to mall?

How much is the fare to the mall?

B 04

Bente pesos yata'.

Twenty pesos I think.

Twenty pesos, I think.

B 05

May pera ka pa ba?

Have money you still [question]?

Do you still have money?

B 06

Oo, may singkwenta pesos pa ako.

Yes, have fifty pesos still I.

Yes, I still have fifty pesos.

Yes/no questions starting with **may** or **meron** can also be answered with **oo**. However, for negative answers, only **wala'** can be used and not **hindi'**.

B 07

Wala' na. Ubos na ang pera ko.

Have none anymore. Used up already the money my.

Not anymore. I've spent all my money.

B 08

dyes, bente, trenta, kwarenta, singkwenta

ten, twenty, thirty, forty, fifty

ten, twenty, thirty, forty, fifty

B 09

sisenta, sitenta, otsenta, nobenta

sixty, seventy, eighty, ninety

sixty, seventy, eighty, ninety

Congratulations for reaching the end of this book! In Course Book 2, the journey continues and we'll focus on the verbs.

Before moving on to Lesson 21, it's a good idea to review Lessons 11–15.

Sa mall

Kailangan kong bumili ng tela.
Anong klaseng tela?
Katsa lang. Para sa project ko.
Ikaw, may bibilhin ka ba?
Wala'. Ubos na kasi ang pera ko.
Naglaro' kasi ako ng computer games kasama ng mga kaibigan ko.
Kaya' pala. Ano ang gagawin mo?
Tatambay na lang ako sa bookstore.
Nasaan pala si Tatay?
Nasa kotse siya. Natutulog siguro.
Sige, magkita' na lang tayo mamaya' ha?

Drills

Kailangan niyang bumili ng gamot.
Hindi' niya kailangang bumili ng pagkain.
Magkano ang pamasahe hanggang sa mall?
Bente pesos yata'.
May pera ka pa ba?
Oo, may singkwenta pesos pa ako.
Wala' na. Ubos na ang pera ko.
dyes, bente, trenta, kwarenta, singkwenta
sisenta, sitenta, otsenta, nobenta

Quick References

Summary of markers and pronouns

		Ang	Ng	Sa
singular	for personal names	si	ni	kay
	for all others	ang (yung)	ng (nung)	sa
plural	for personal names	sina	nina	kina
	for all others	ang mga (yung mga)	ng mga (nung mga)	sa mga

	Ang	Ng	Sa
I, my etc.	ako	ko	(sa) <u>a</u>kin
you, your etc. (singular)	ikaw, ka	mo	(sa) iyo
he/she, his/her etc.	siya	niya	(sa) kanya
we, our etc. (excluding you)	kami	<u>na</u>min	(sa) <u>a</u>min
we, our etc. (including you)	<u>ta</u>yo	<u>na</u>tin	(sa) <u>a</u>tin
you, your etc. (plural)	kayo	ninyo / niyo	(sa) inyo
they, their etc.	sila	nila	(sa) kanila
this etc. (near me)	ito	nito	<u>di</u>to / <u>ri</u>to
that etc. (near you)	iyan	niyan	diyan / riyan
that/it etc. (far from you and me)	iyon	niyon / noon	doon / roon

these etc. (near me)	ang mga ito itong mga ito	ng mga ito nitong mga ito	sa mga ito
those etc. (near you)	ang mga iyan iyang mga iyan	ng mga iyan niyang mga iyan	sa mga iyan
those/they etc. (far from you and me)	ang mga iyon iyong mga iyon	ng mga iyon niyong / noong mga iyon	sa mga iyon

In this book, Ang phrase, Ng phrase and Sa phrase are used to refer to the three marker and pronoun groups.

phrase	refers to—	examples
Ang phrase	• phrases introduced by an Ang marker, • Ang pronouns	ang ba<u>bae</u> si Bill siya ito
Ng phrase	• phrases introduced by a Ng marker, • Ng pronouns	ng ba<u>bae</u> ni Bill niya nito
Sa phrase	• phrases introduced by a Sa marker, • Sa pronouns	sa ba<u>bae</u> kay Bill kanya <u>di</u>to

Order of enclitic words

When there are two or more enclitic words in a sentence, they generally appear in the following order:

1	2				3	4
ka	na/pa	naman	pala		niya	ako
ko	man	daw/raw	kaya'		namin	siya
mo	nga'	po'/ho'	muna		natin	kami
	din/rin	ba	tuloy		ninyo	tayo
	lang		kasi		nila	kayo
			yata'			sila
			sana		kita	

Note: Enclitic particles (column 2) are generally used in the order given above, i.e. **na** comes before **man**, **lang** before **naman** etc.

www.ingramcontent.com/pod-product-compliance
Lightning Source LLC
Chambersburg PA
CBHW042042240426
43667CB00047B/2944